WOLF

I0758918

AN ADULT COLORING BOOK

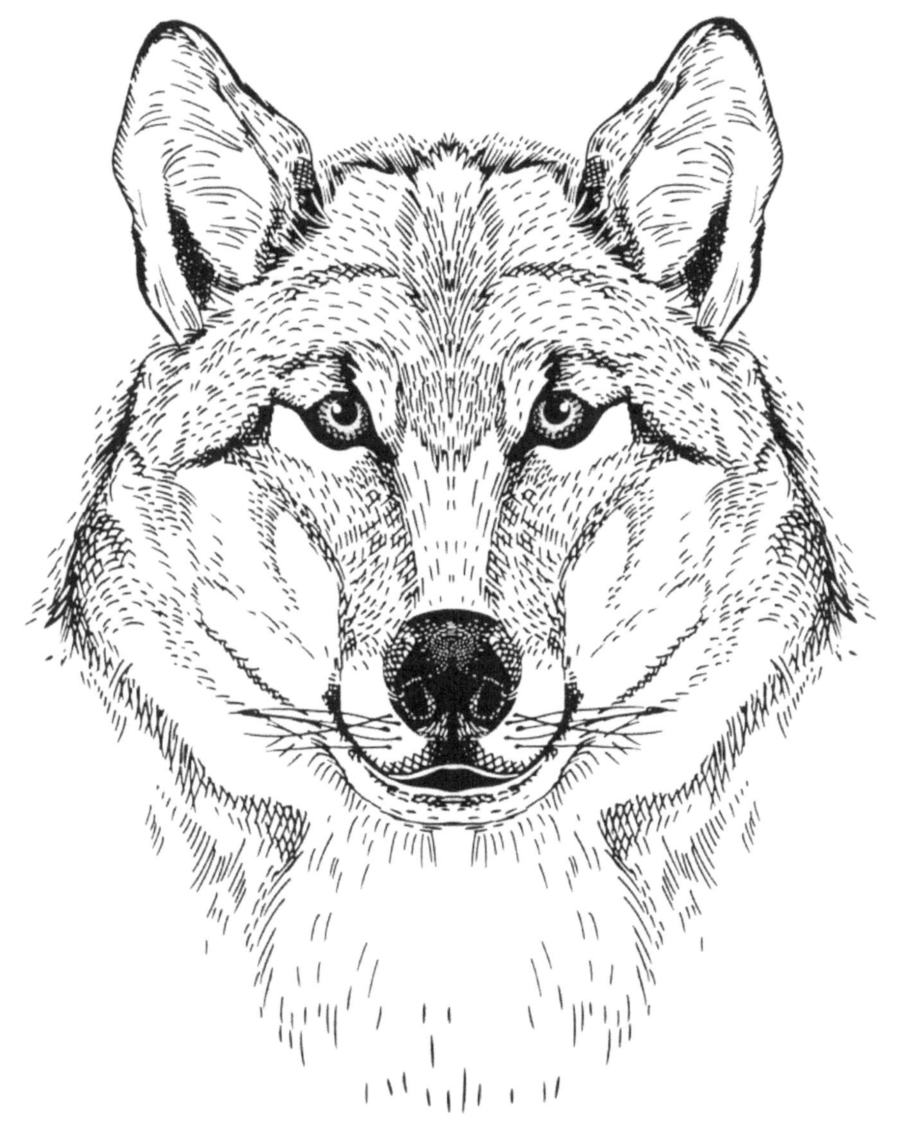

52 Wolf Coloring Pages

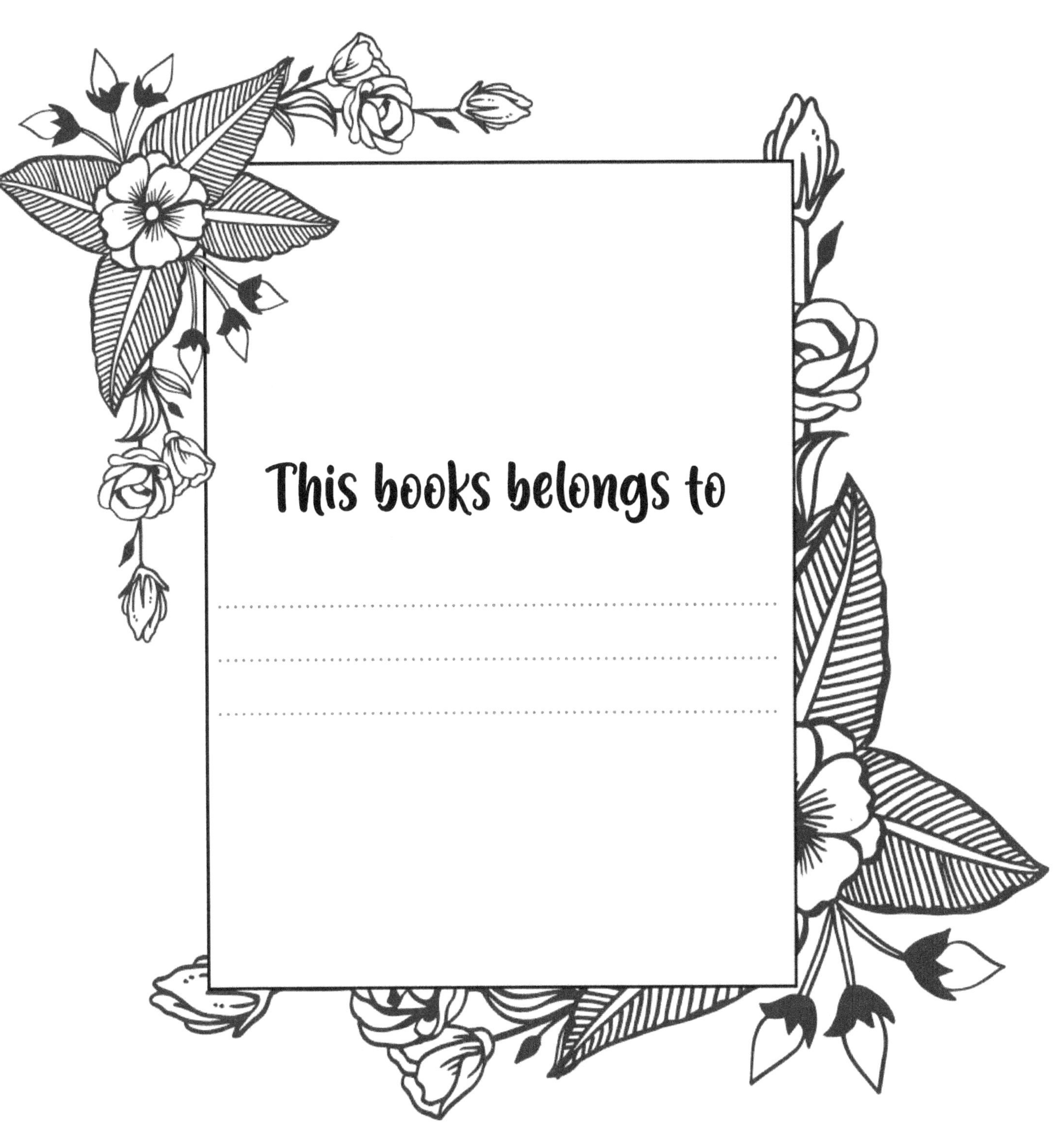
This books belongs to

Color Test Page

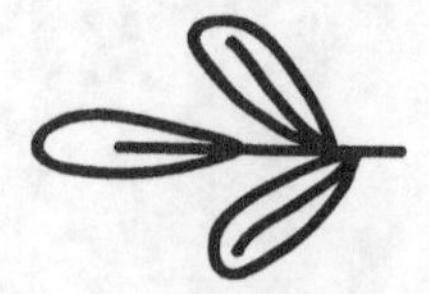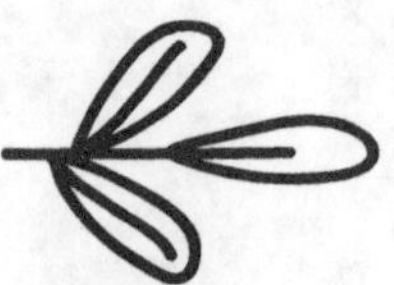

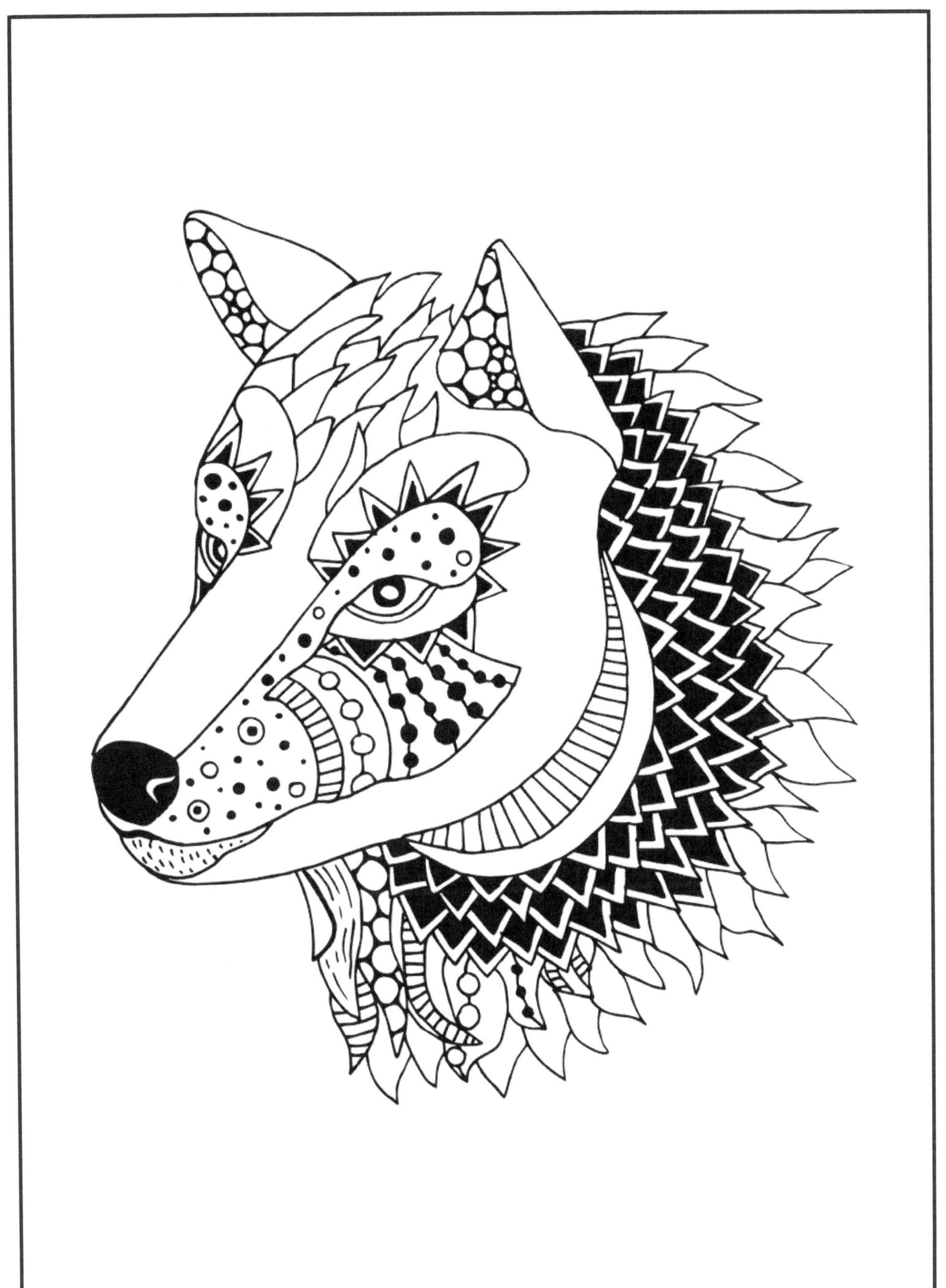

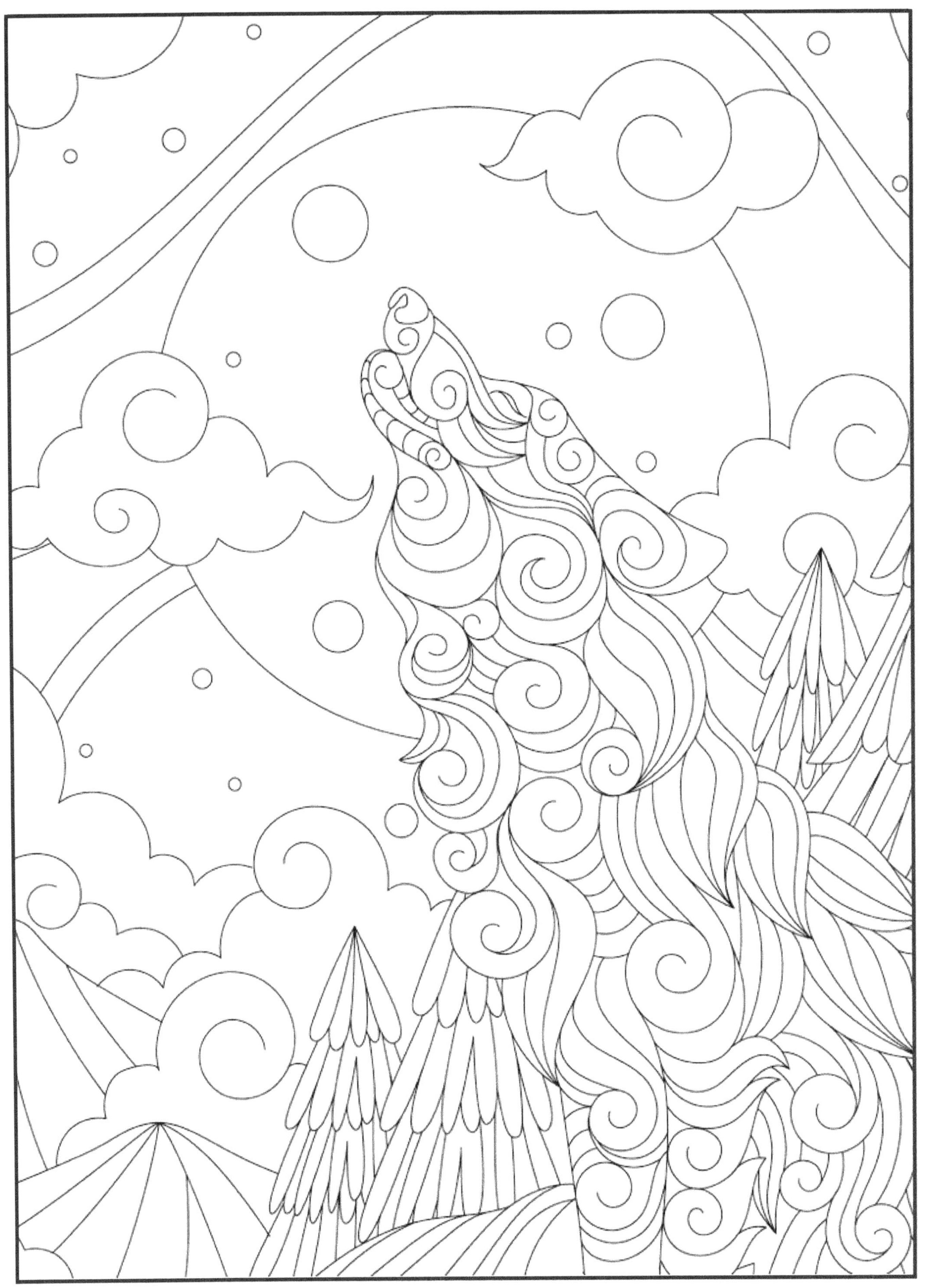

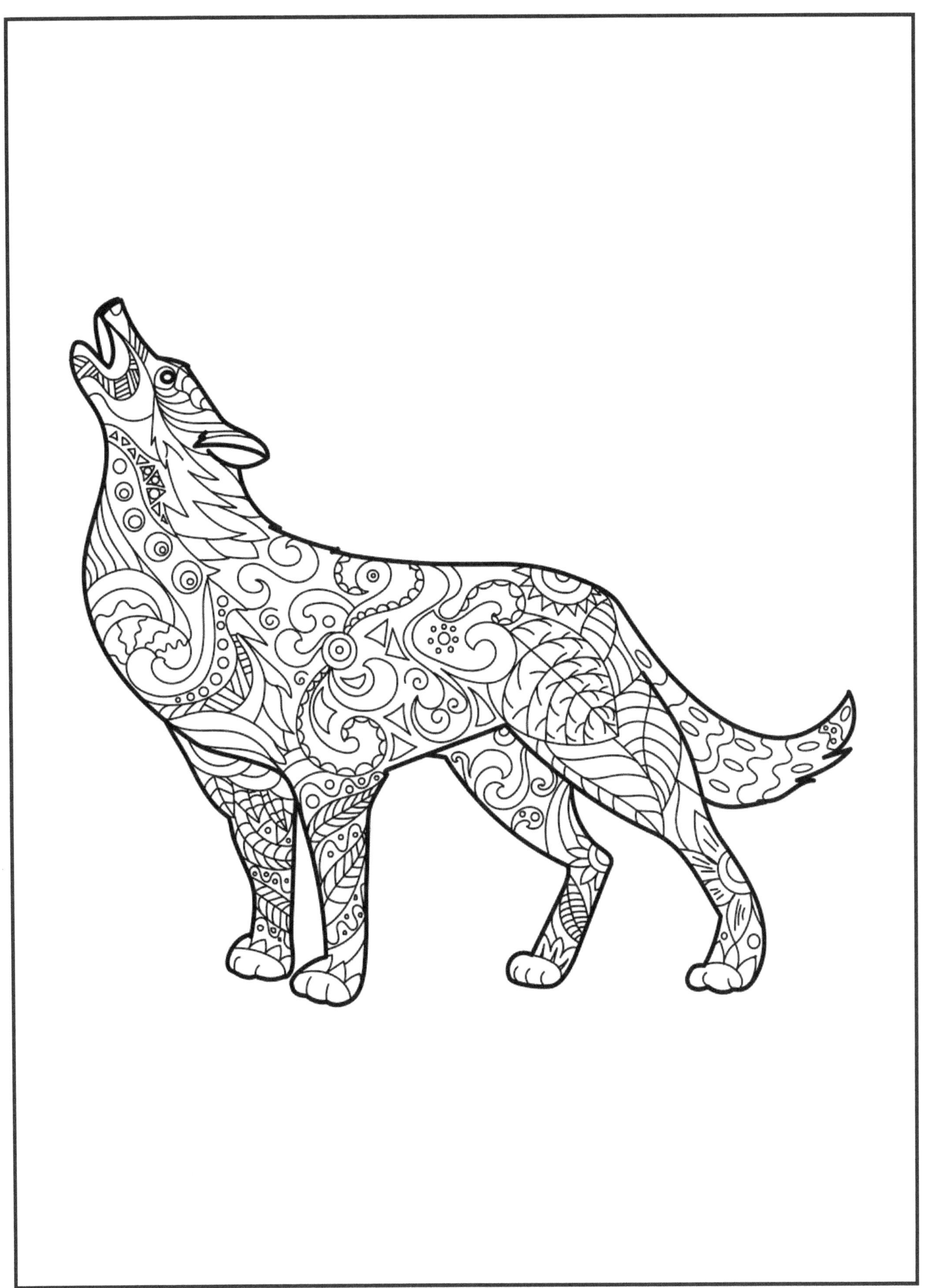

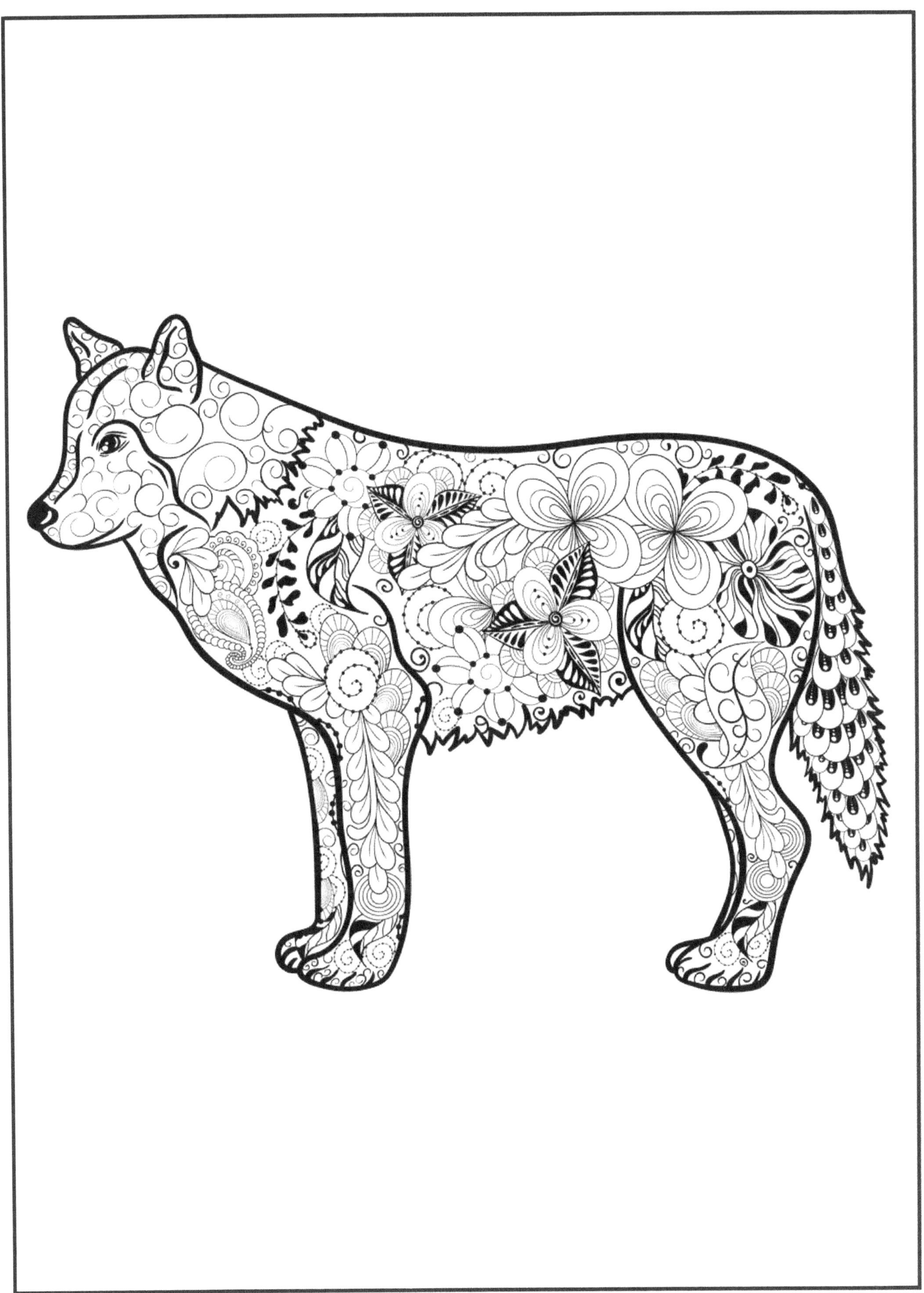

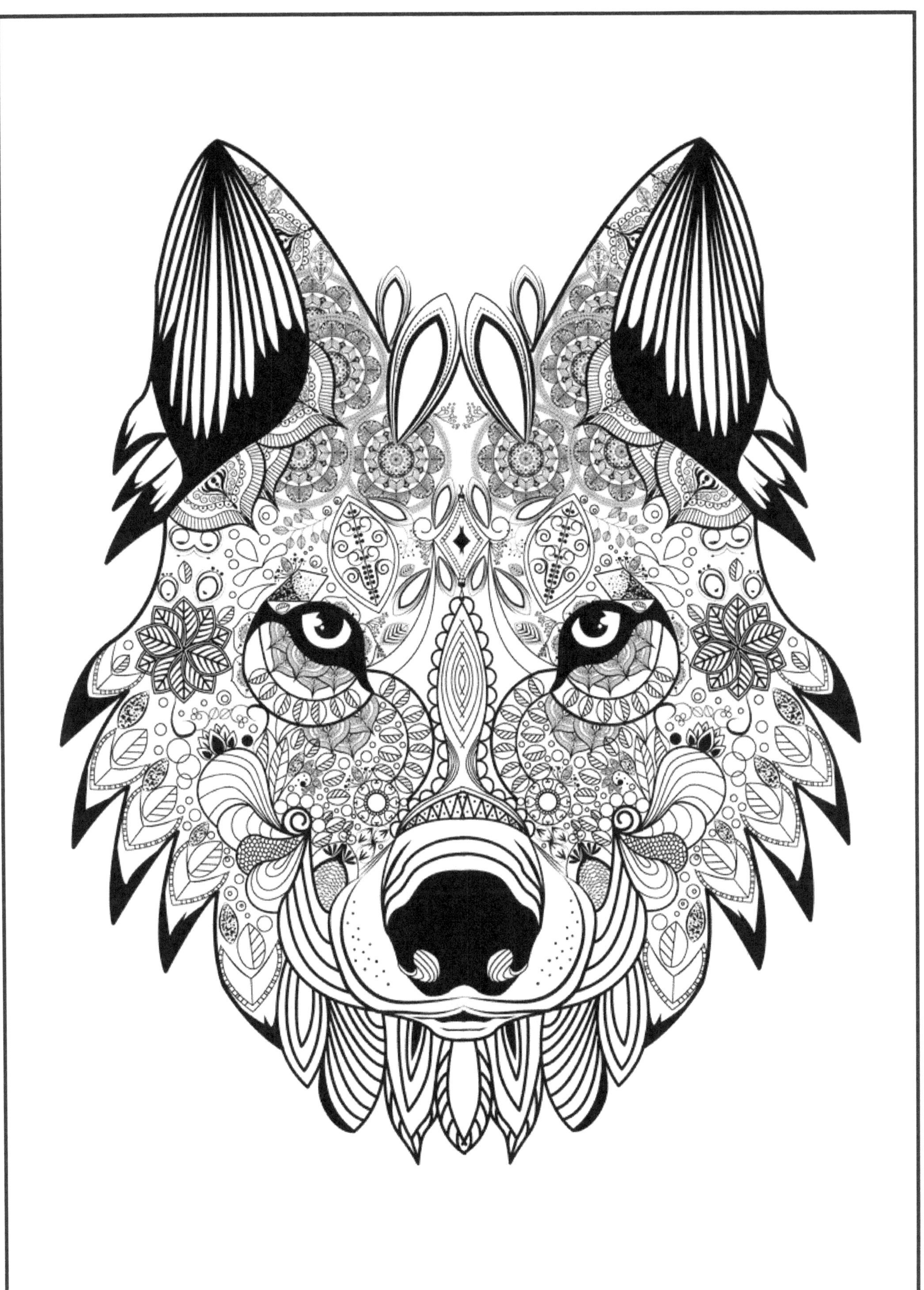

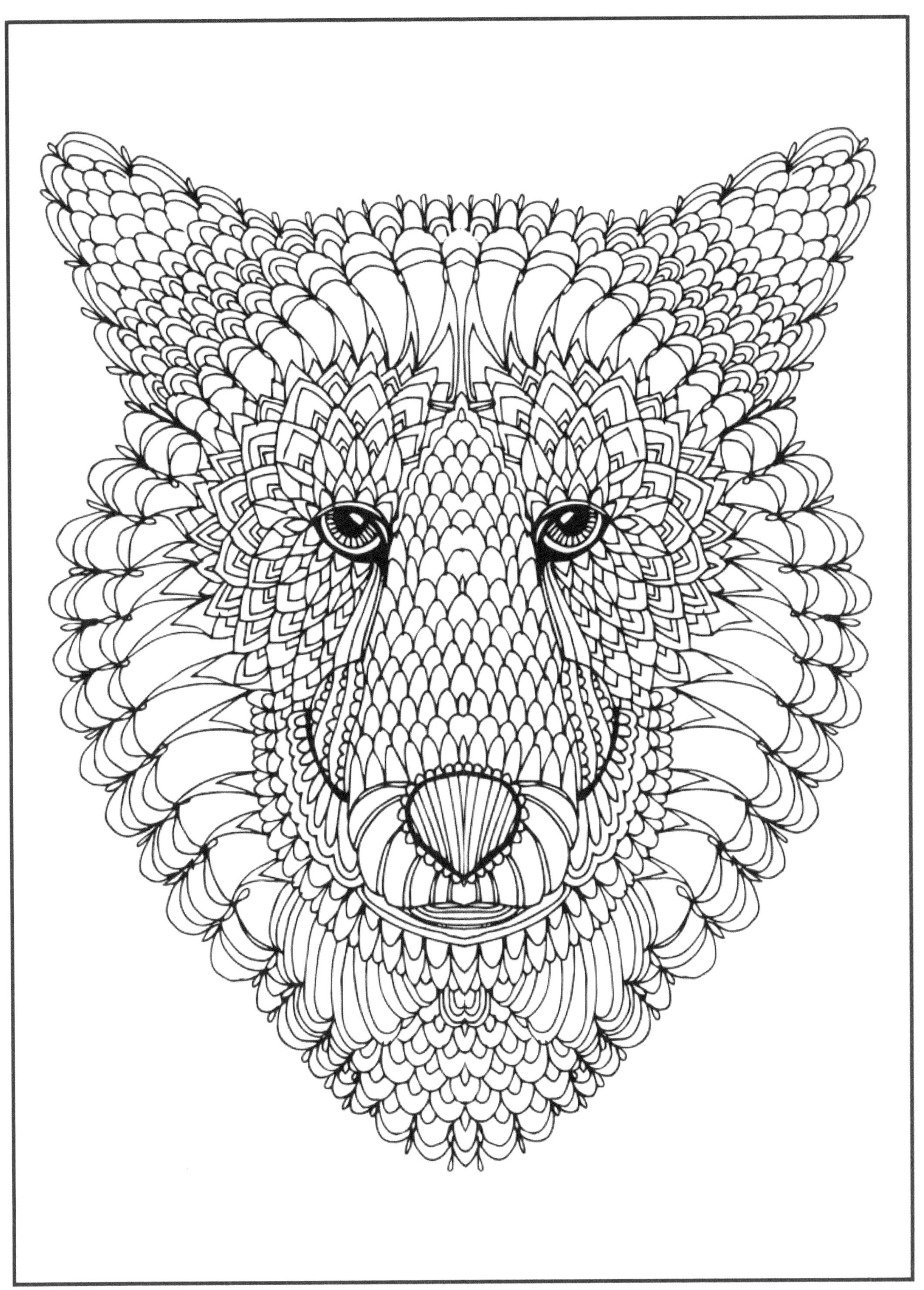

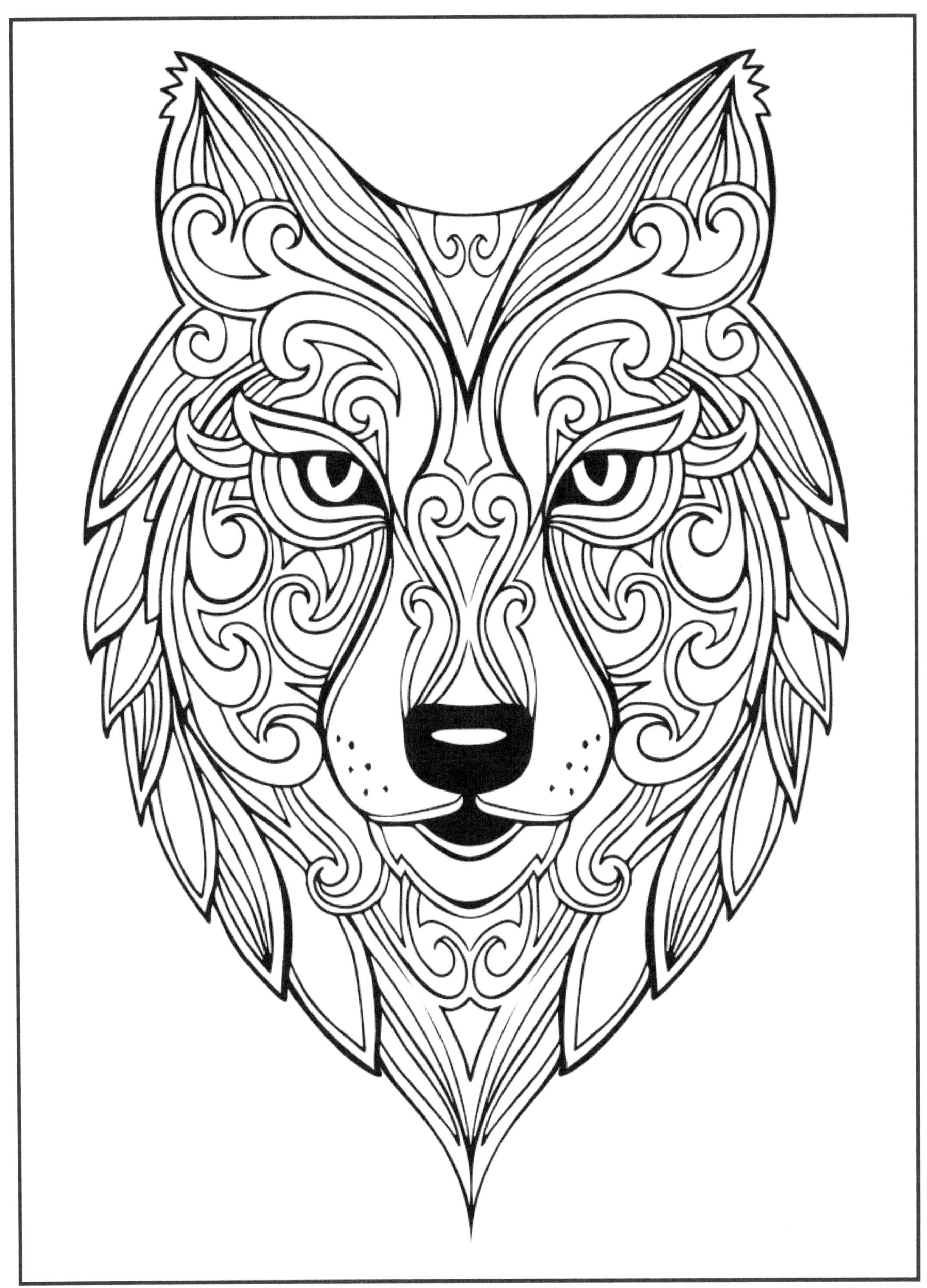

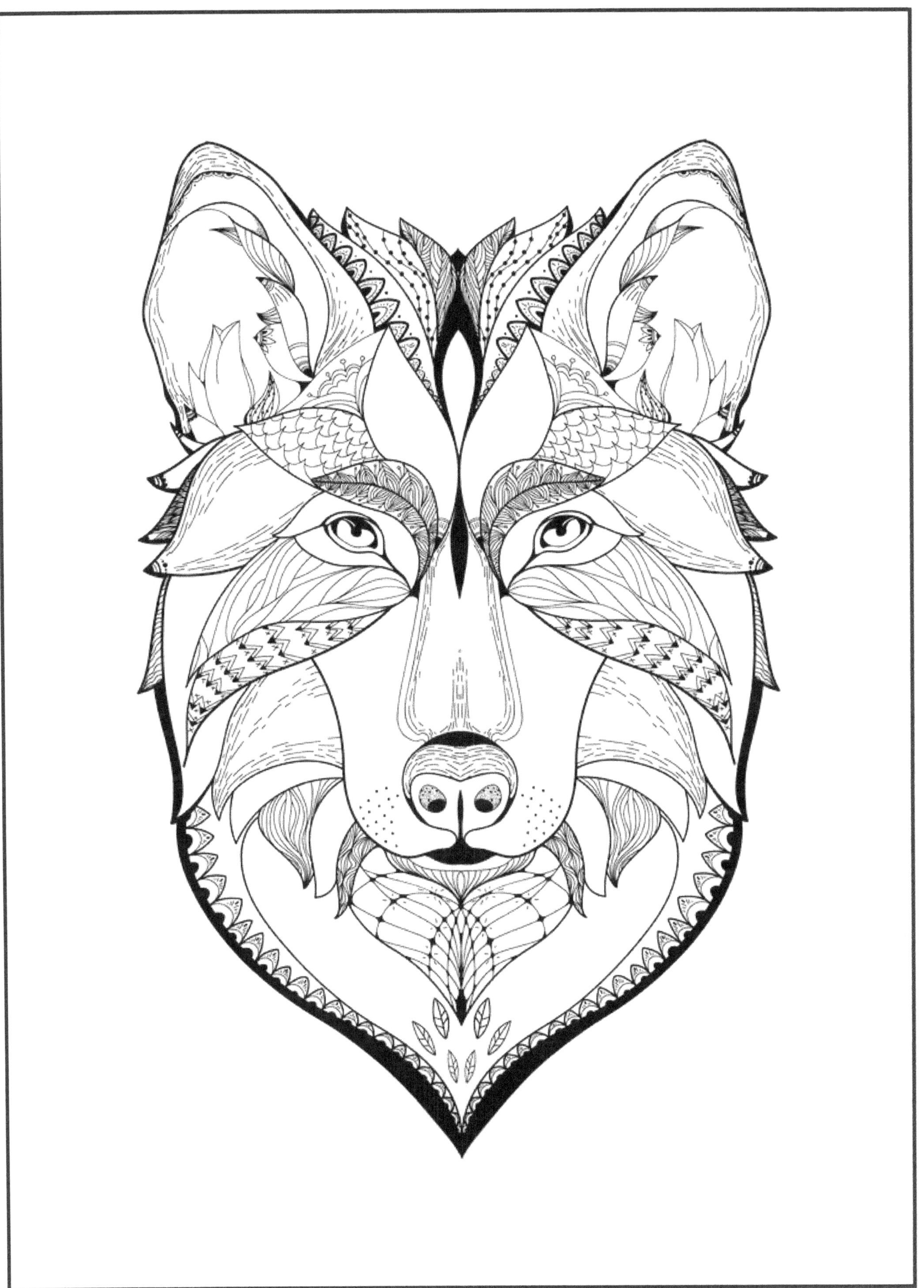

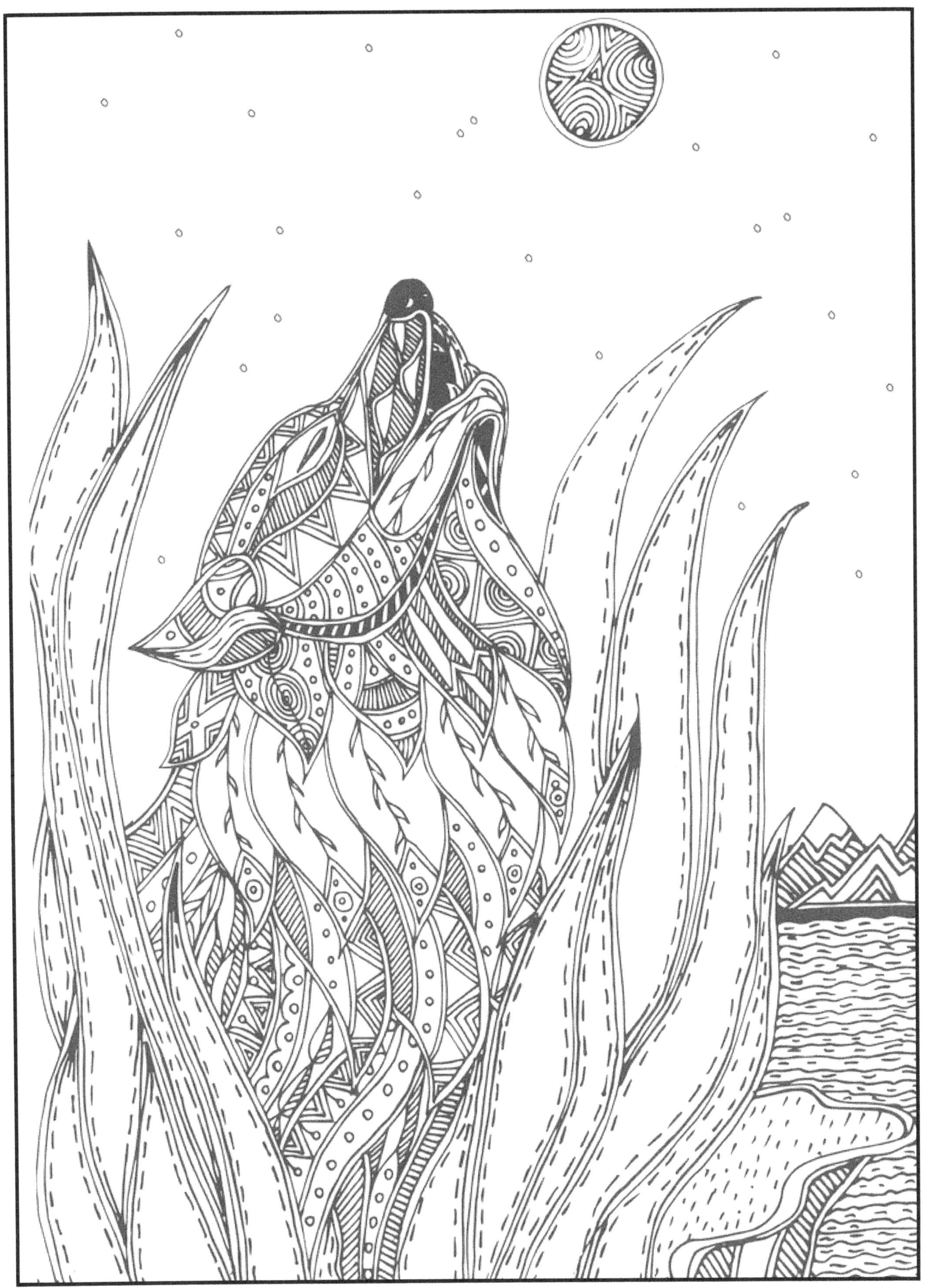

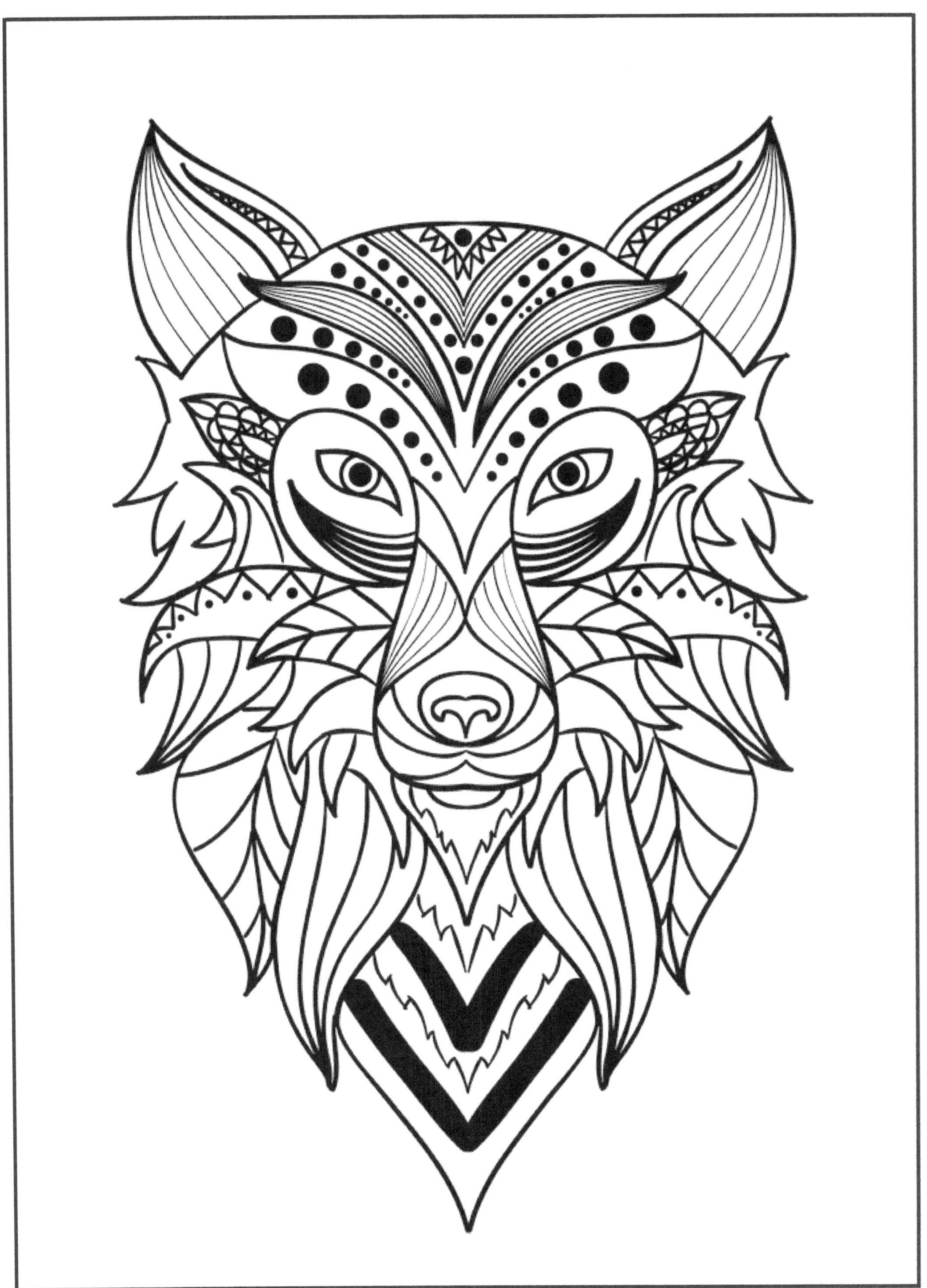

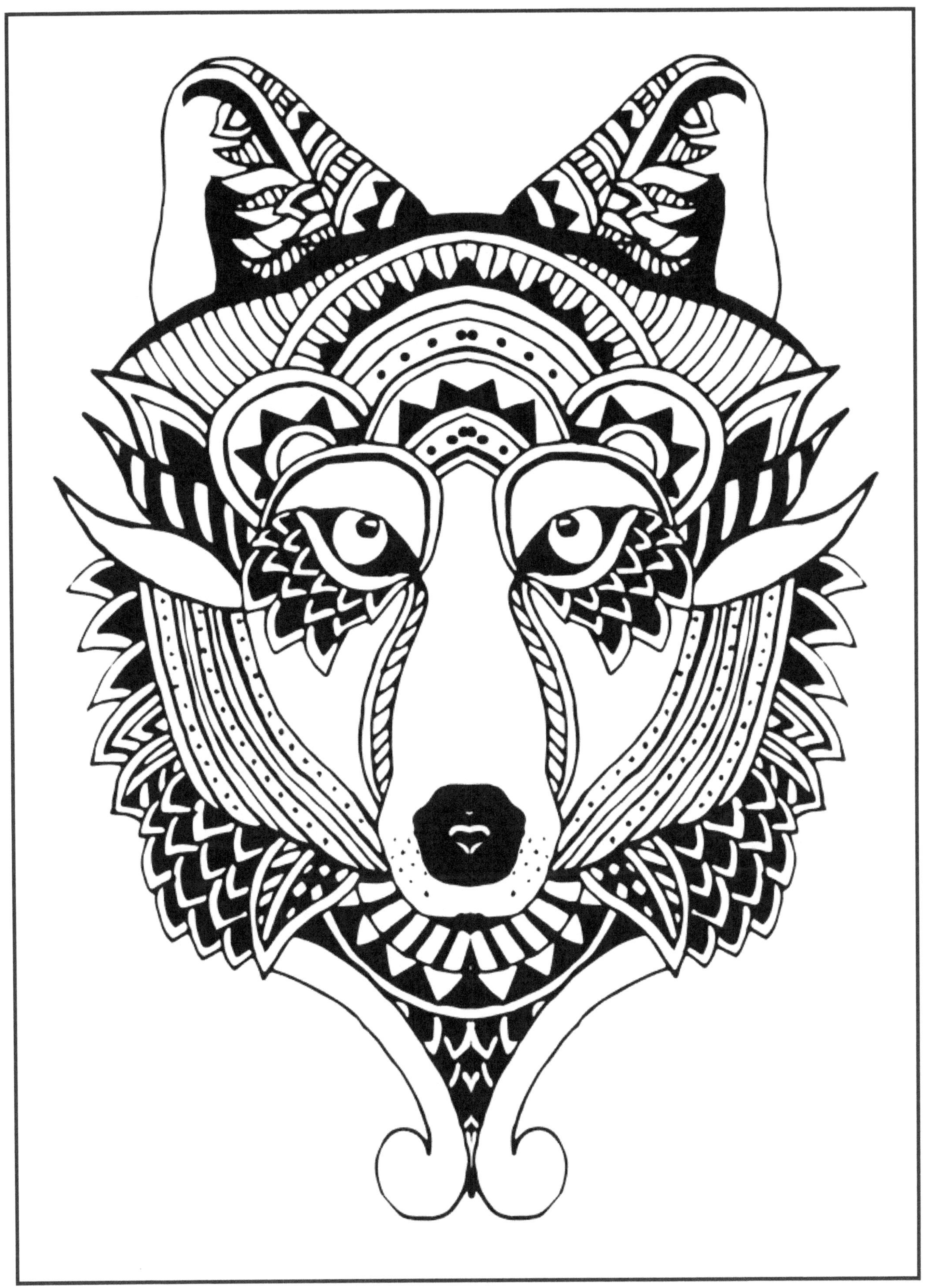

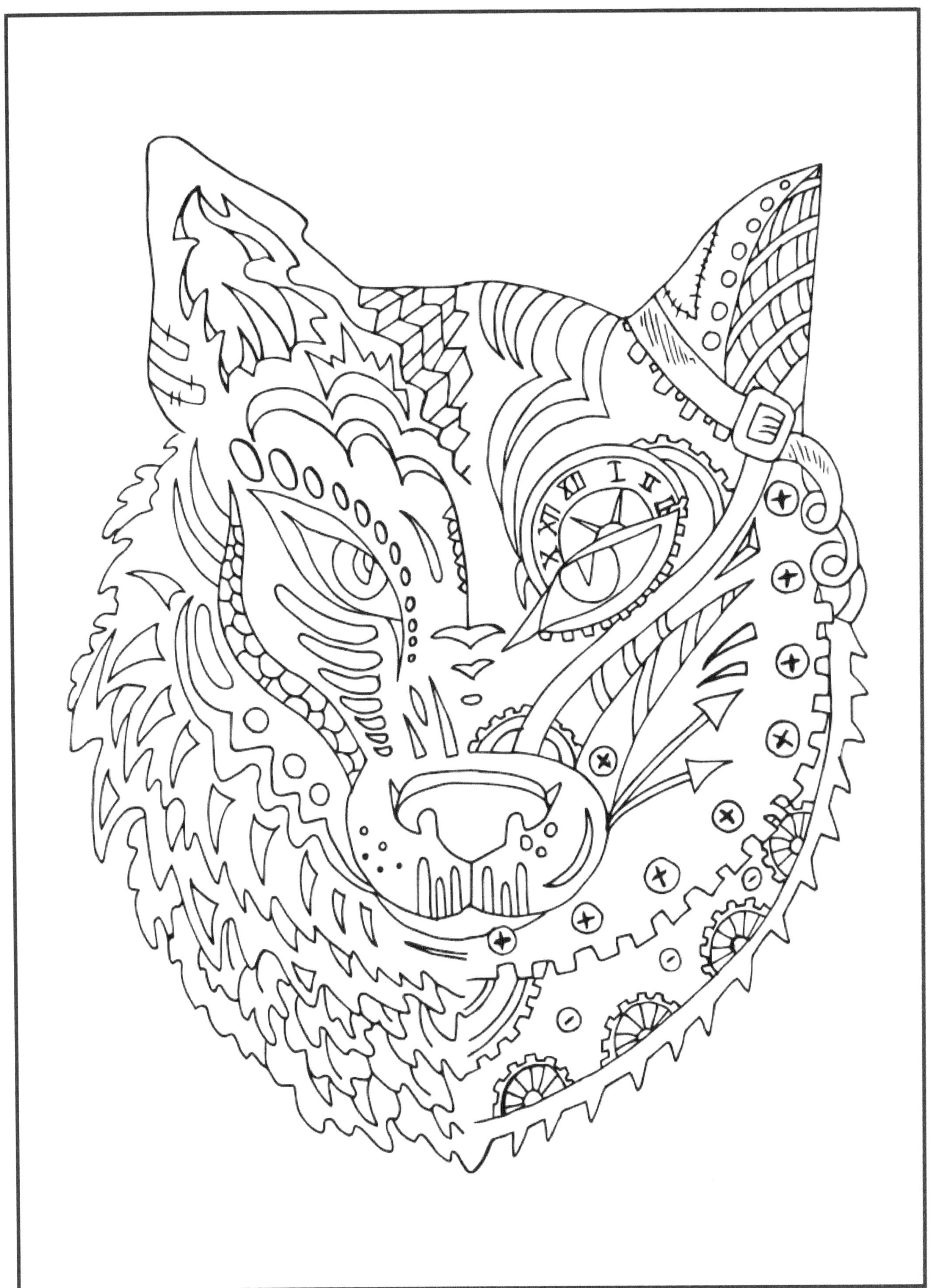

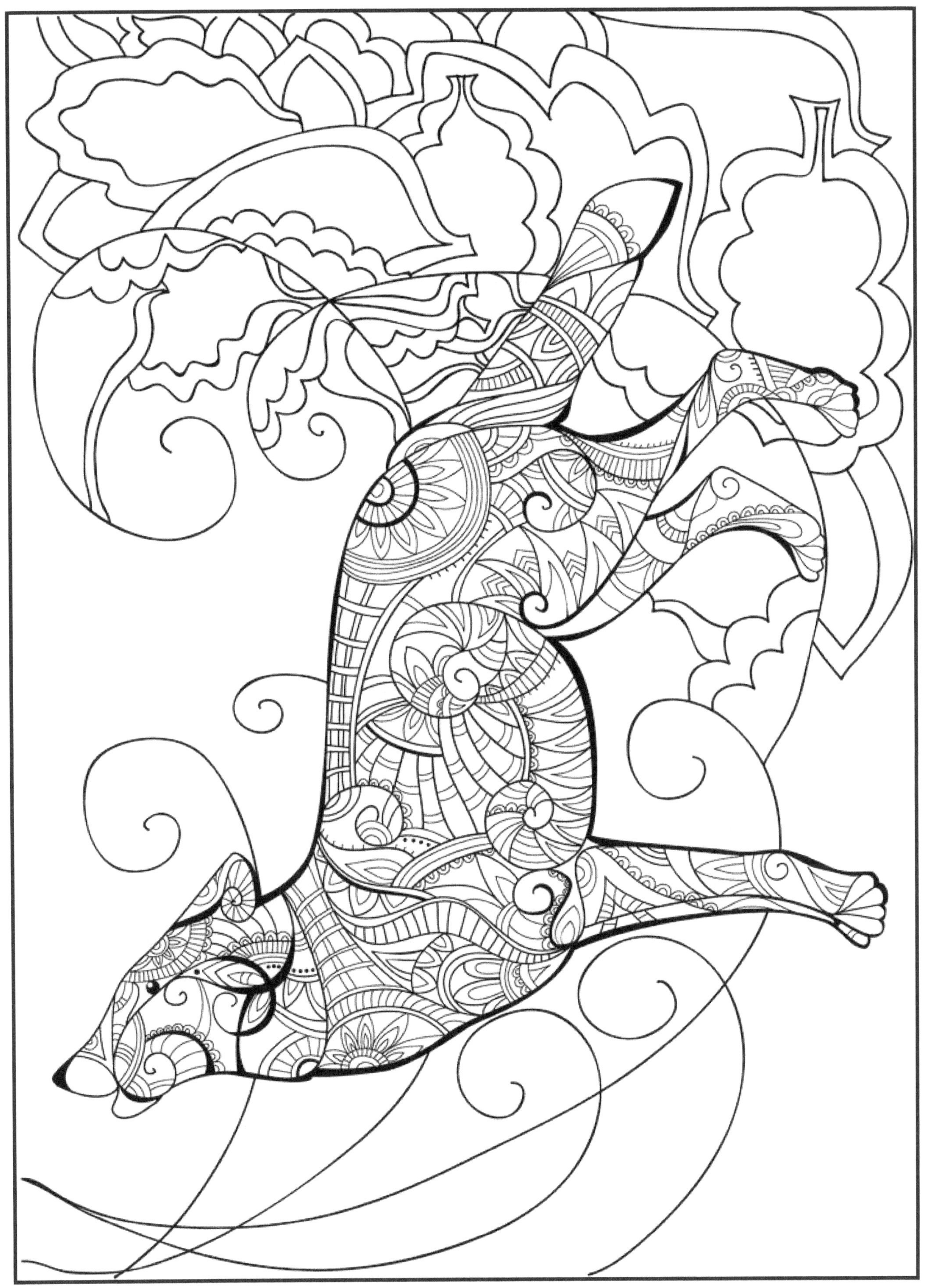

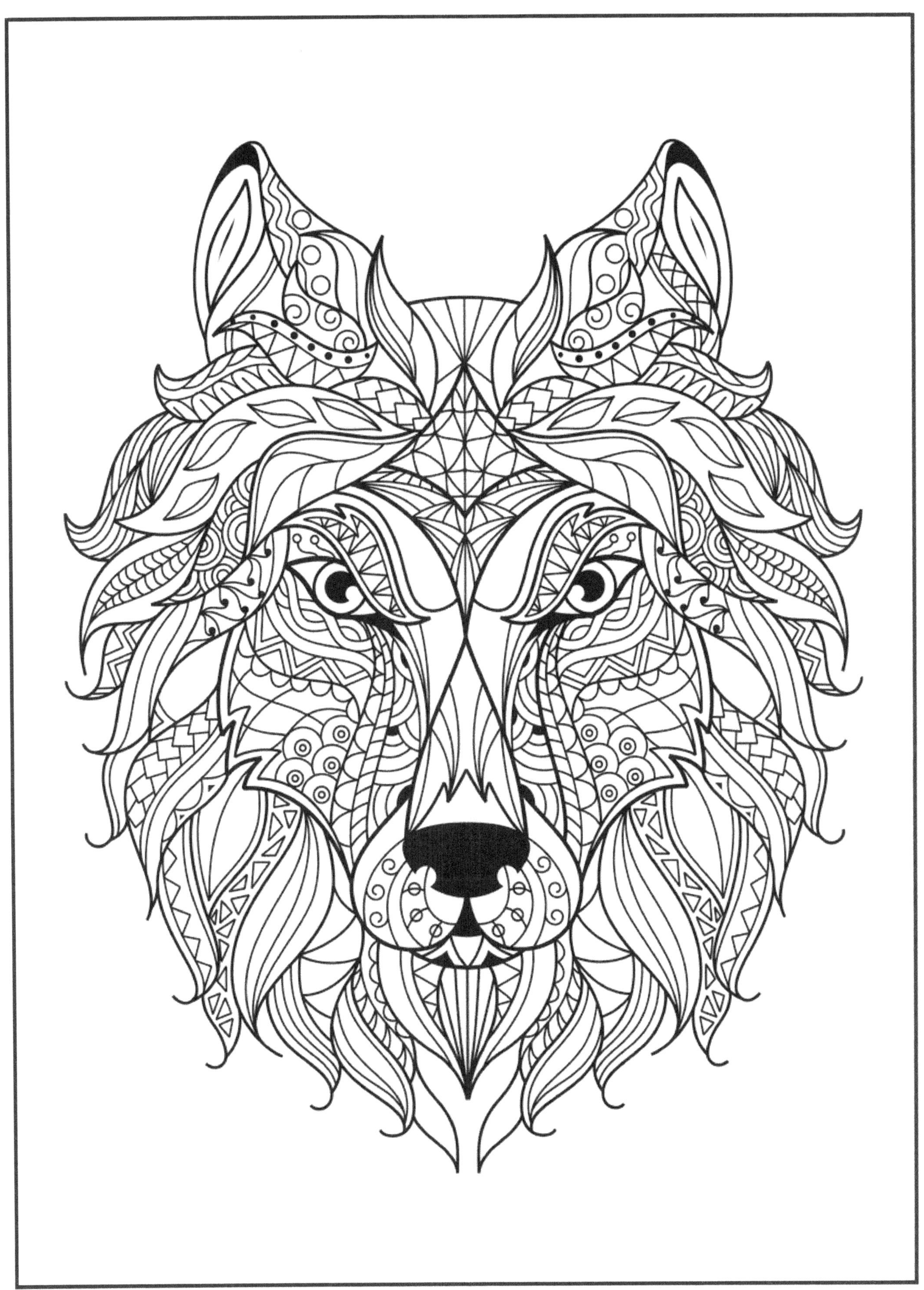

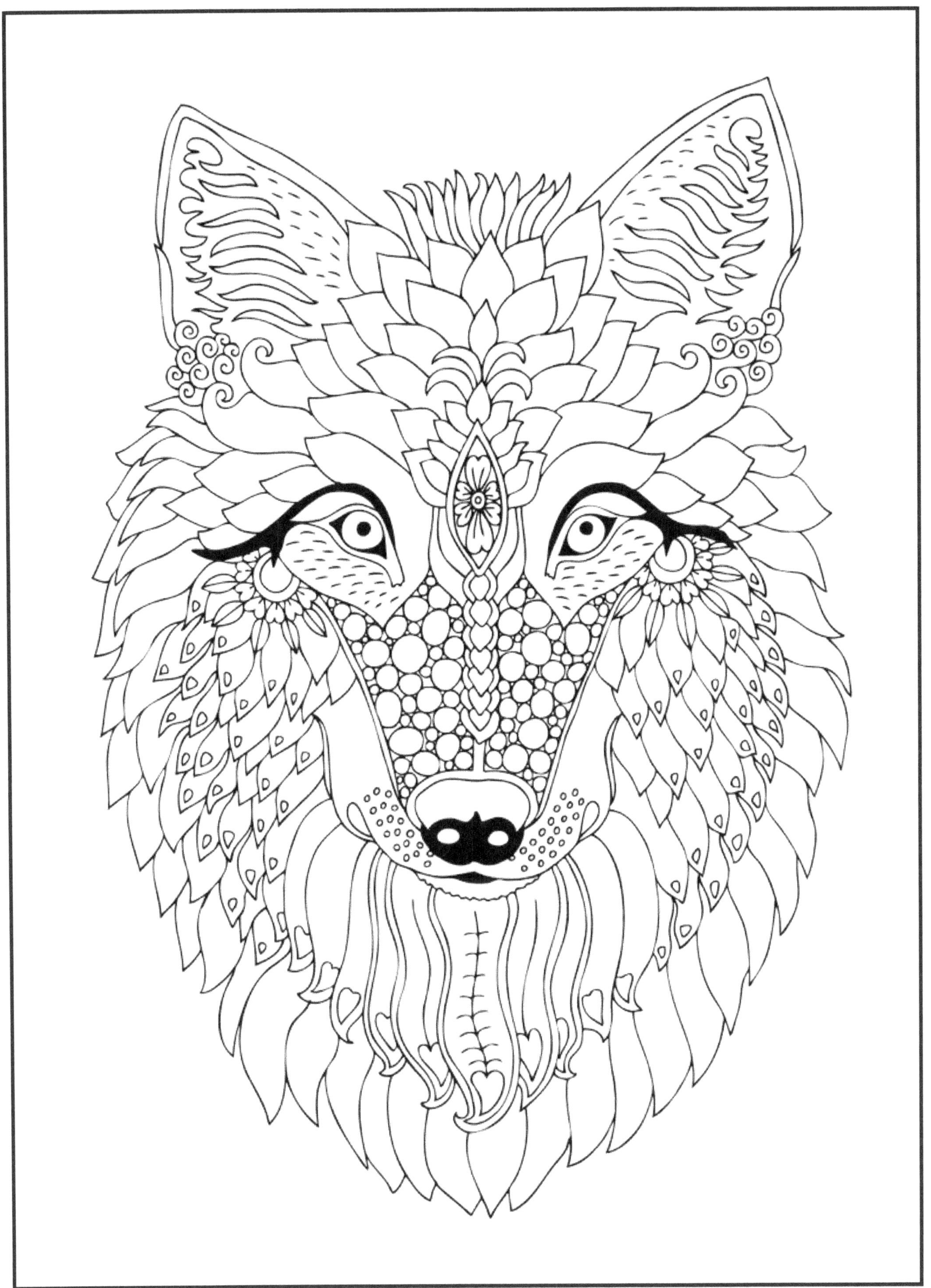

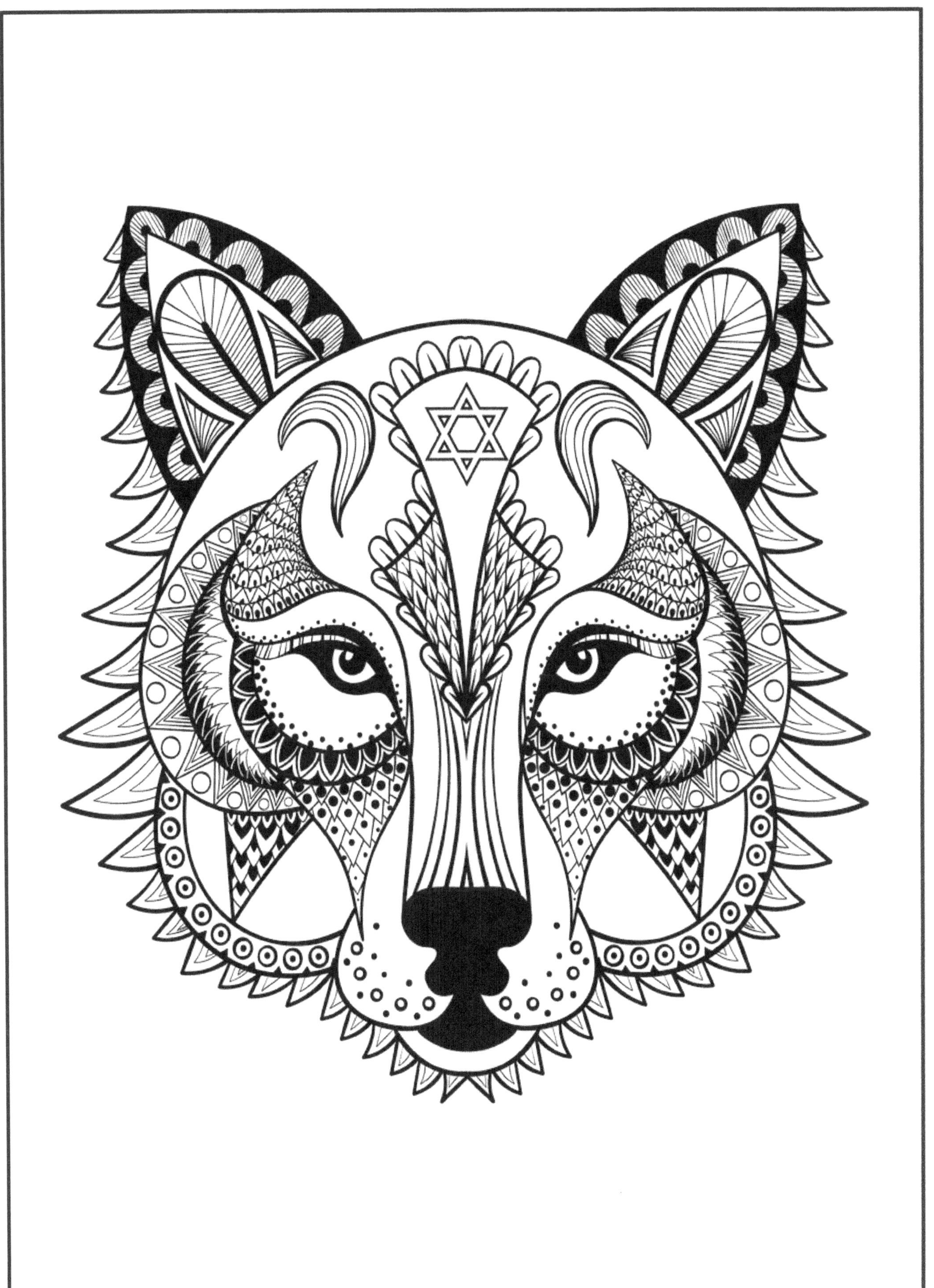

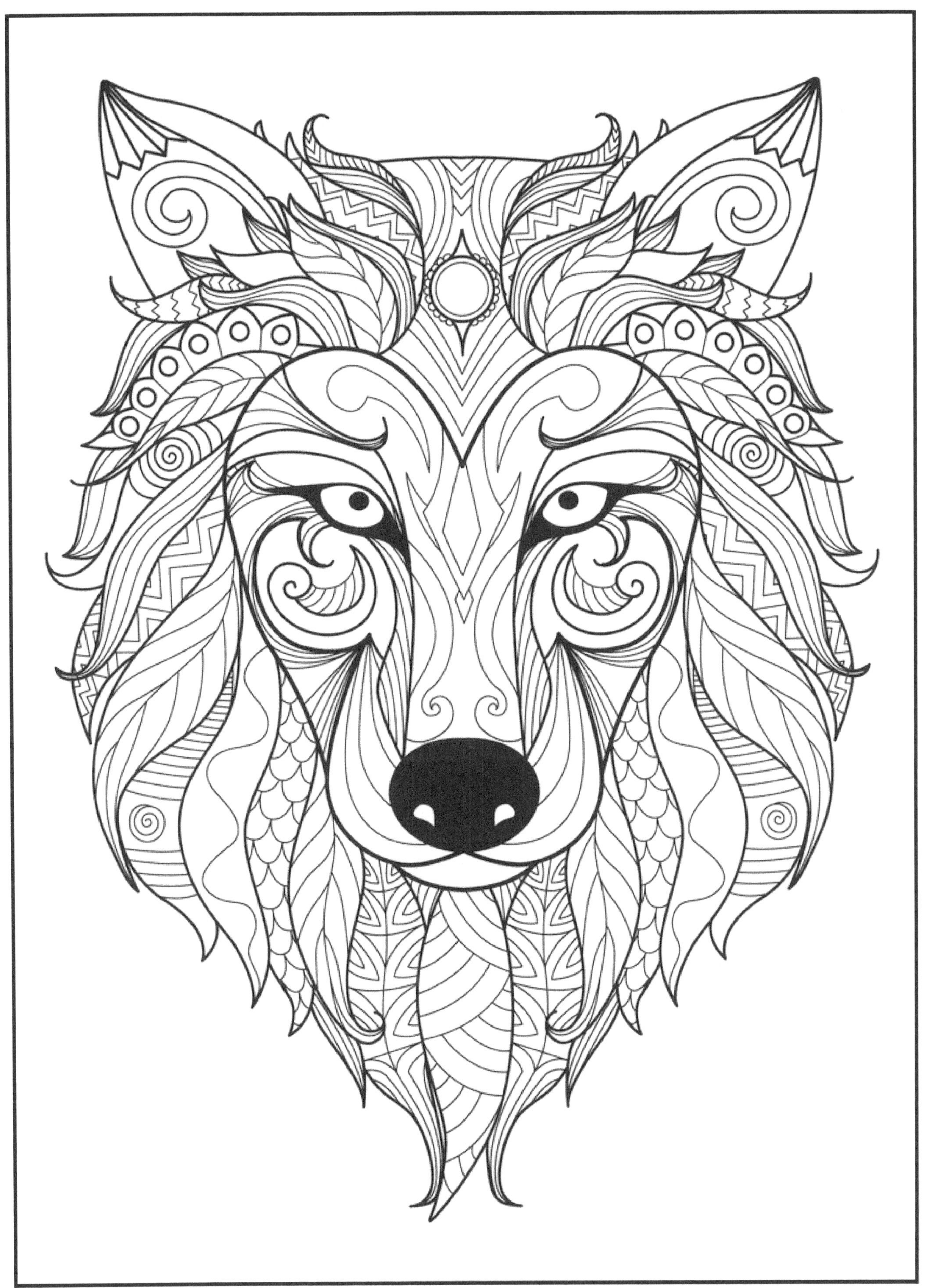

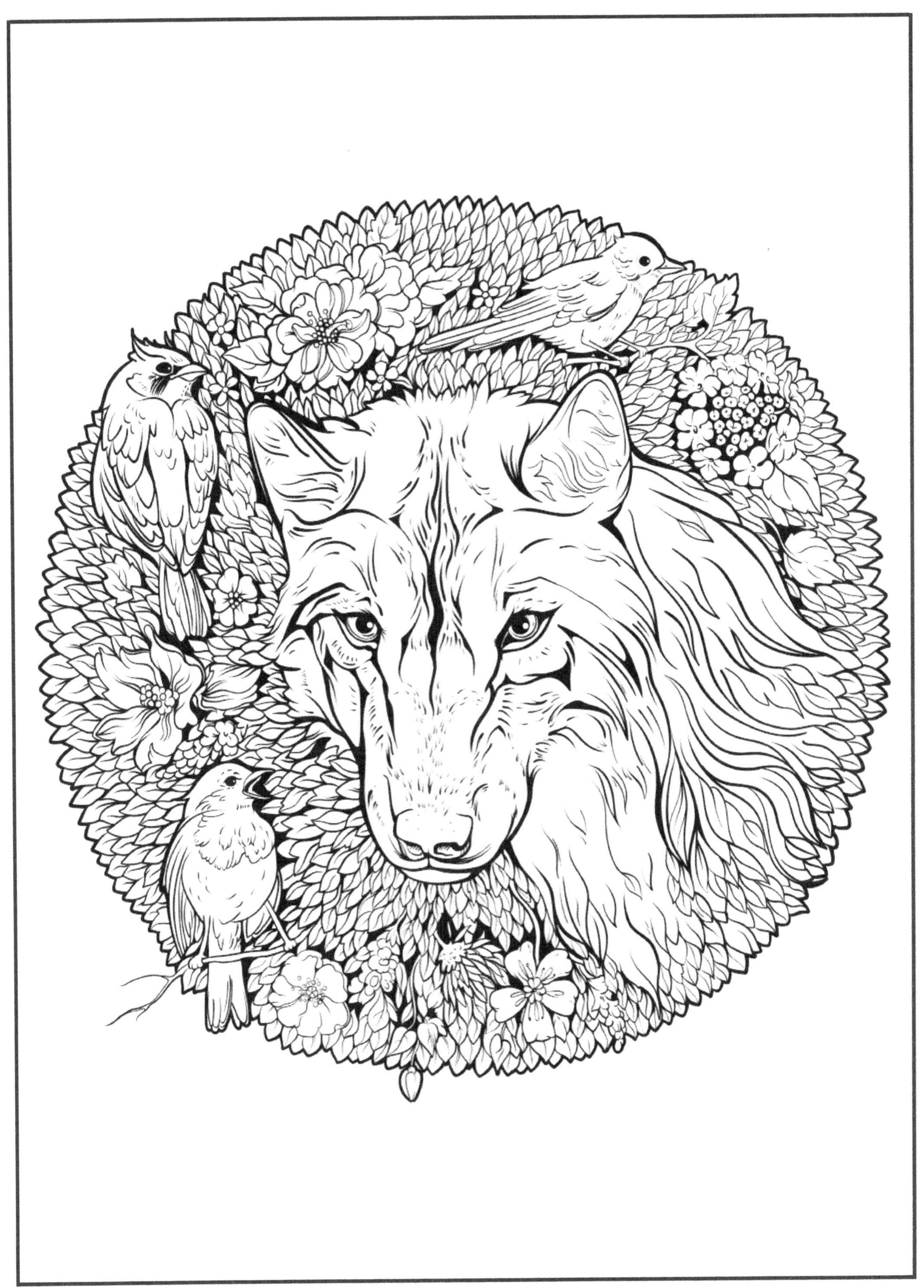

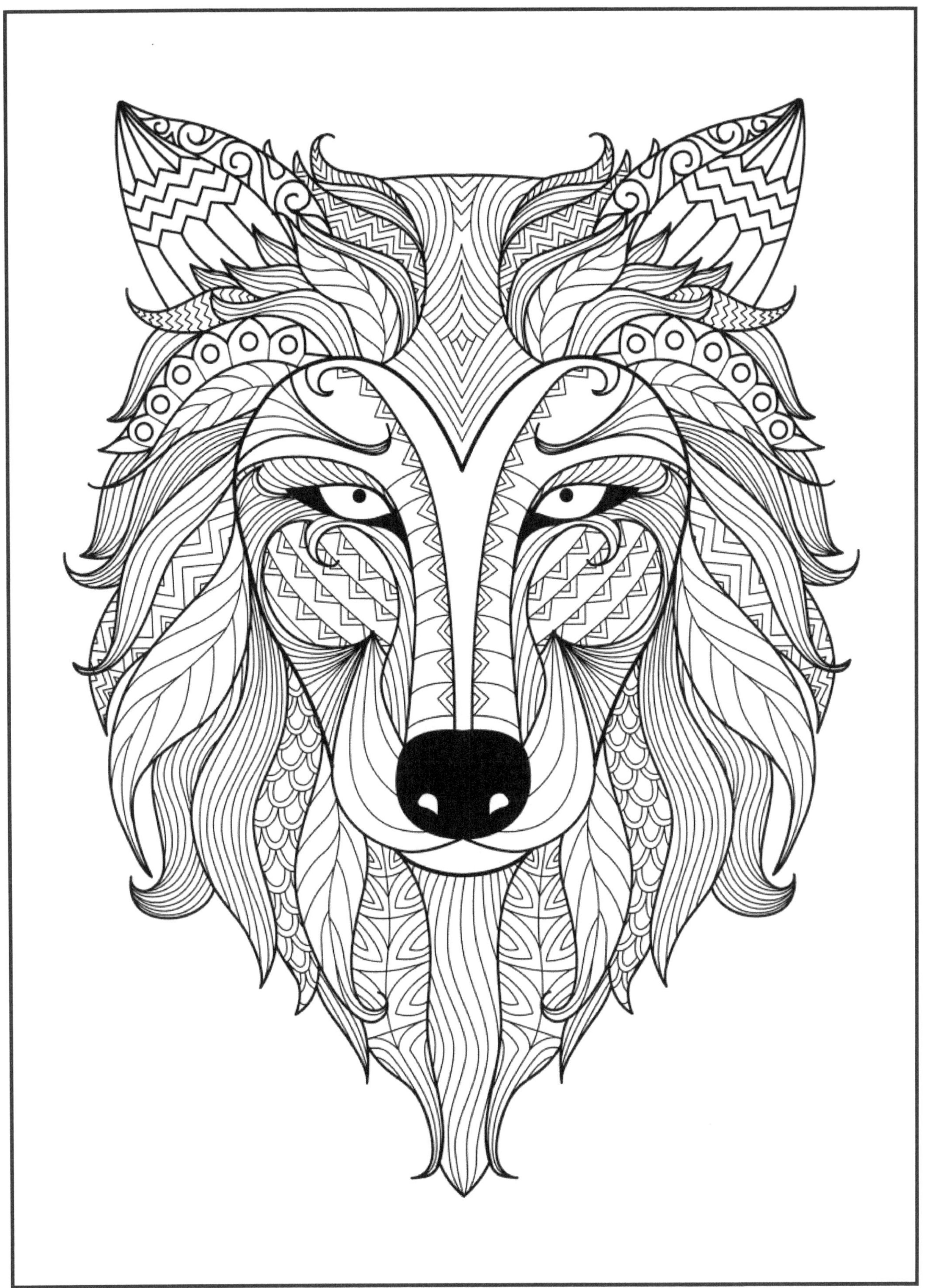

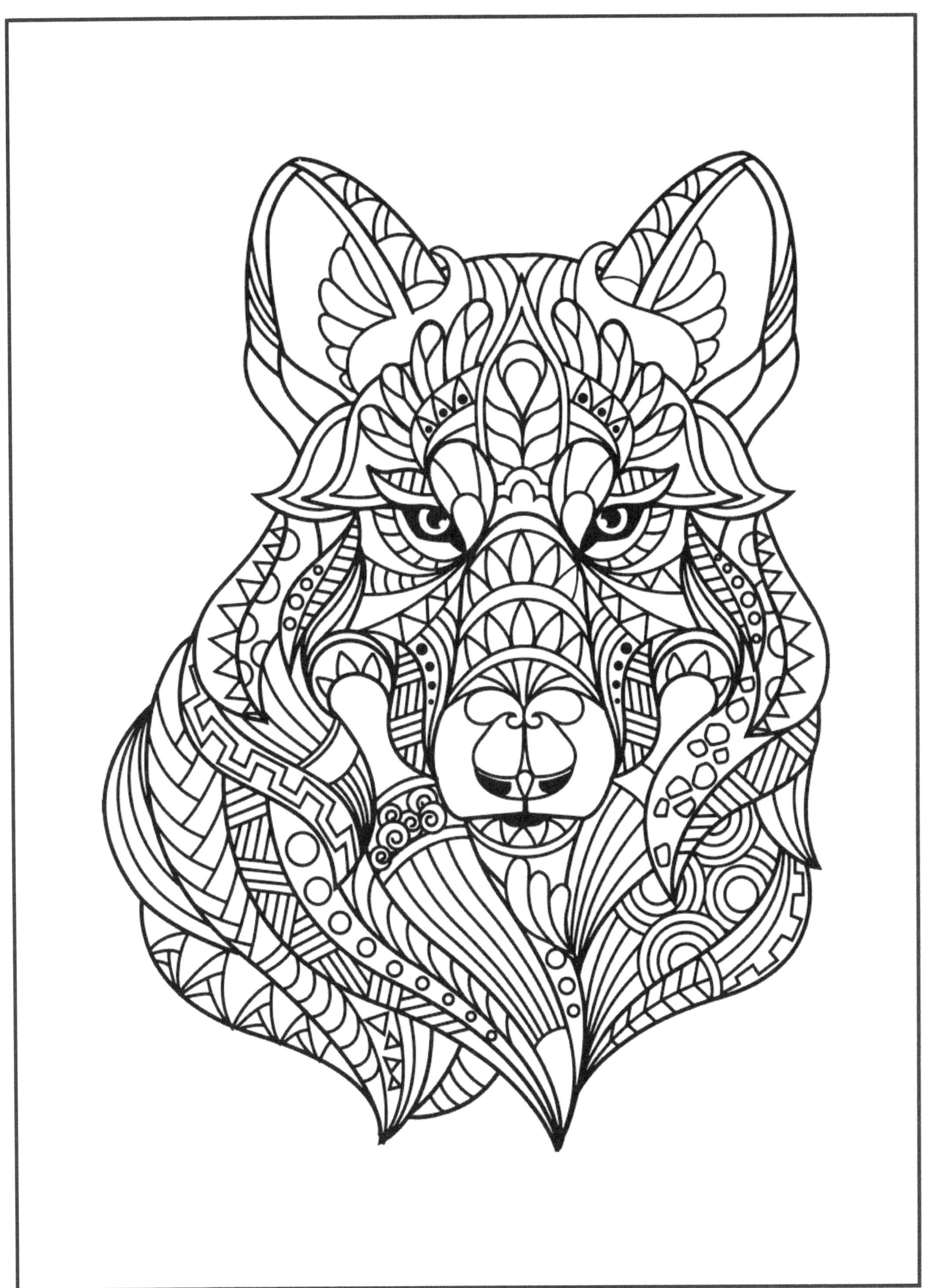

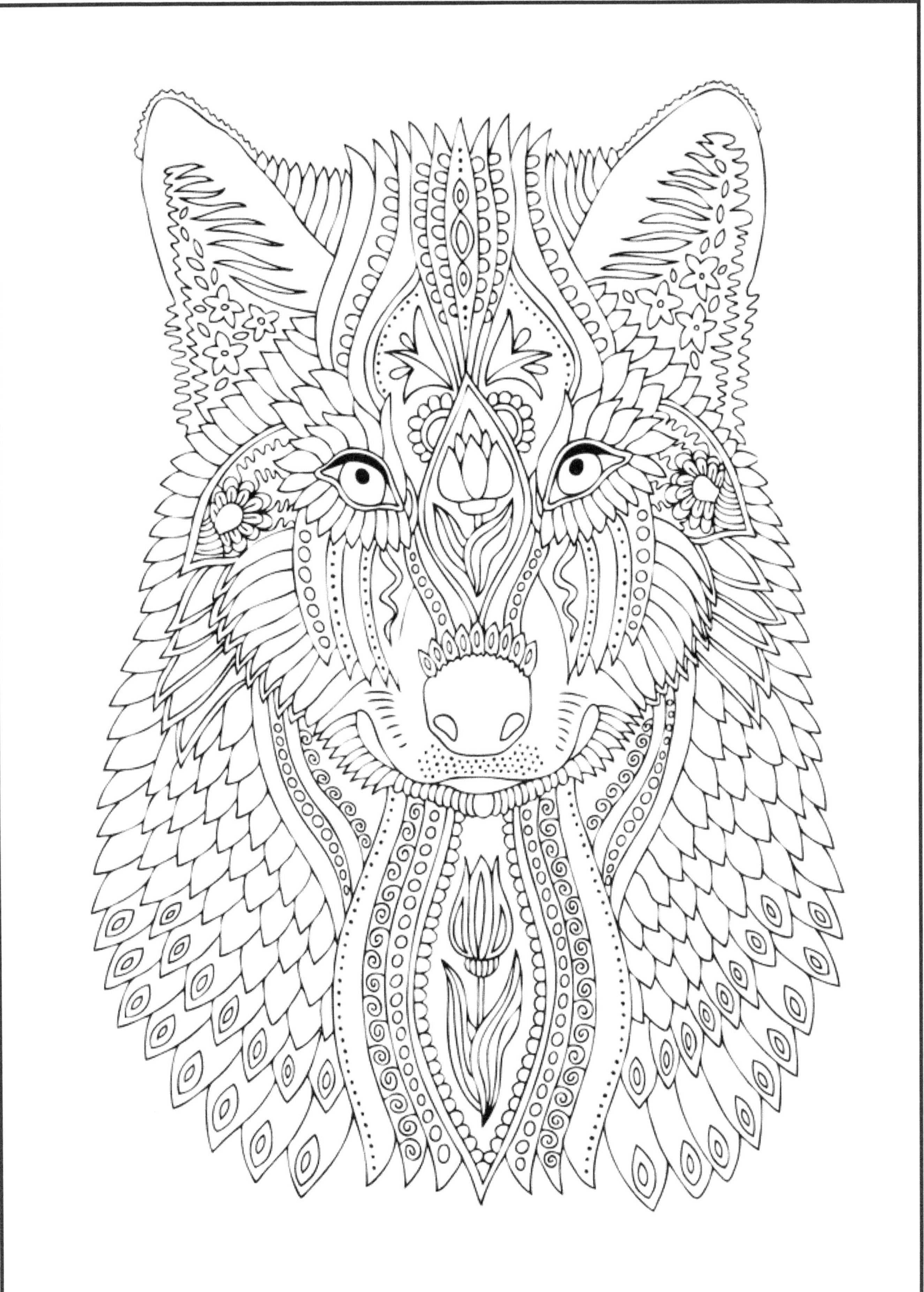

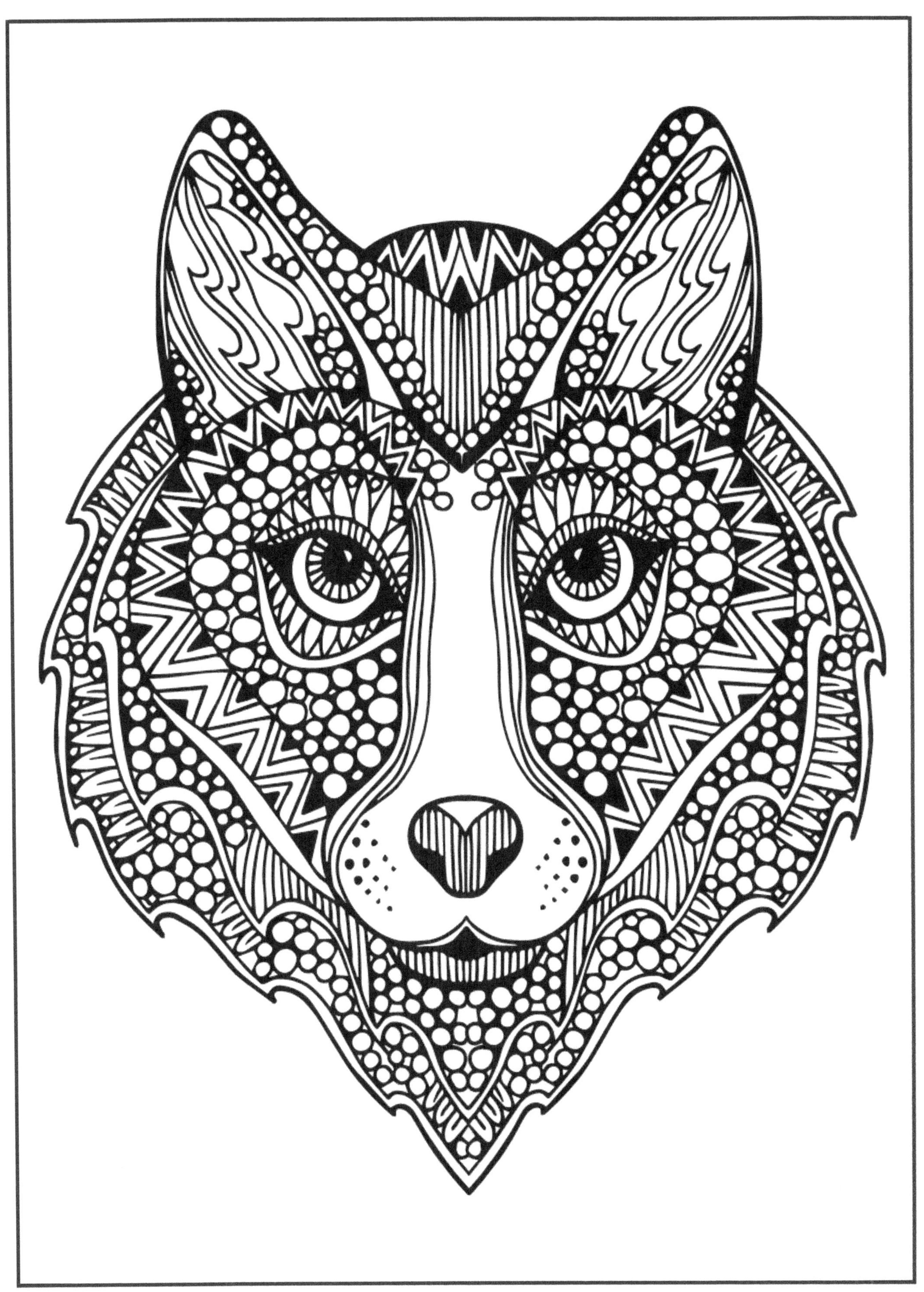

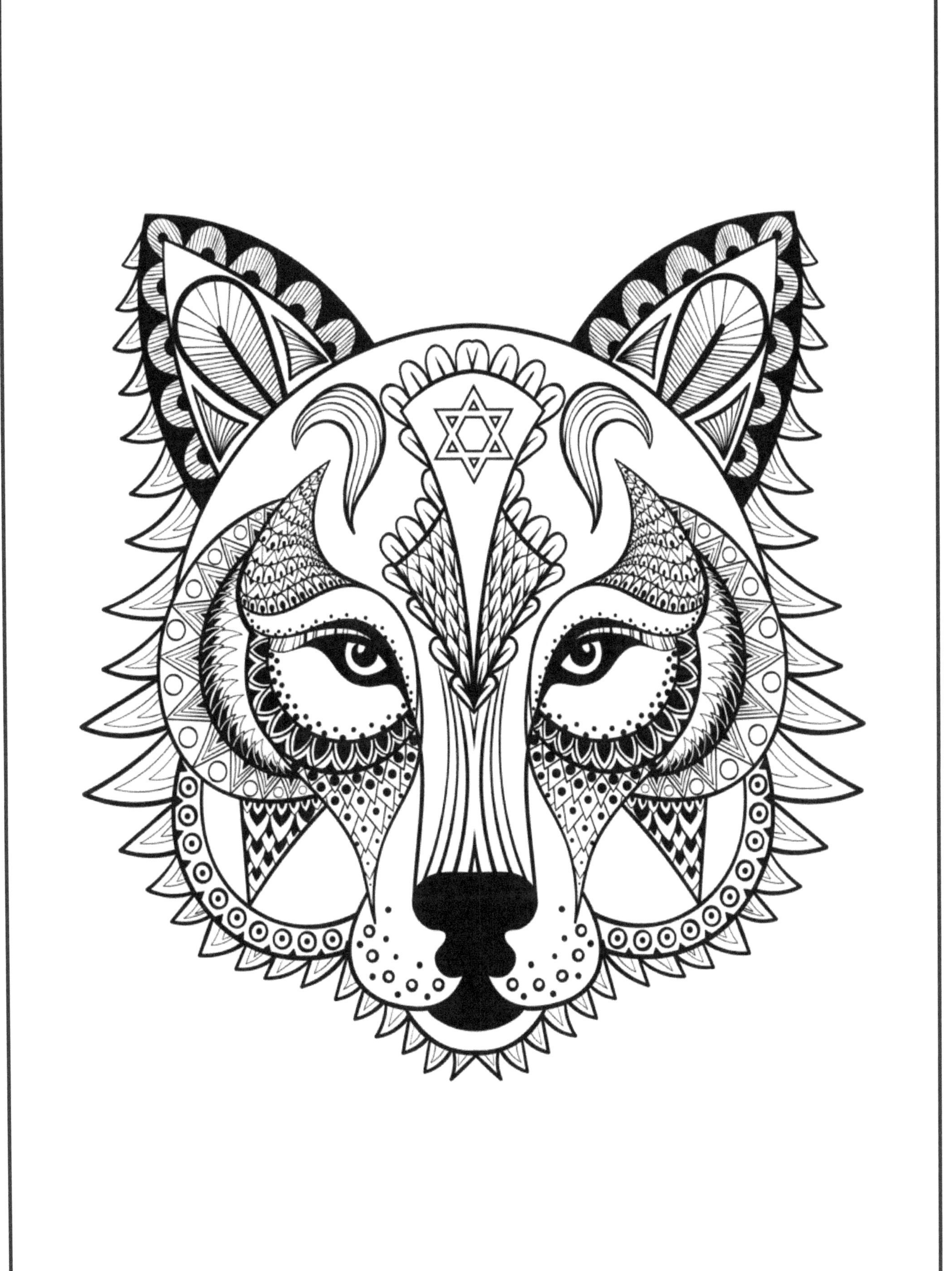

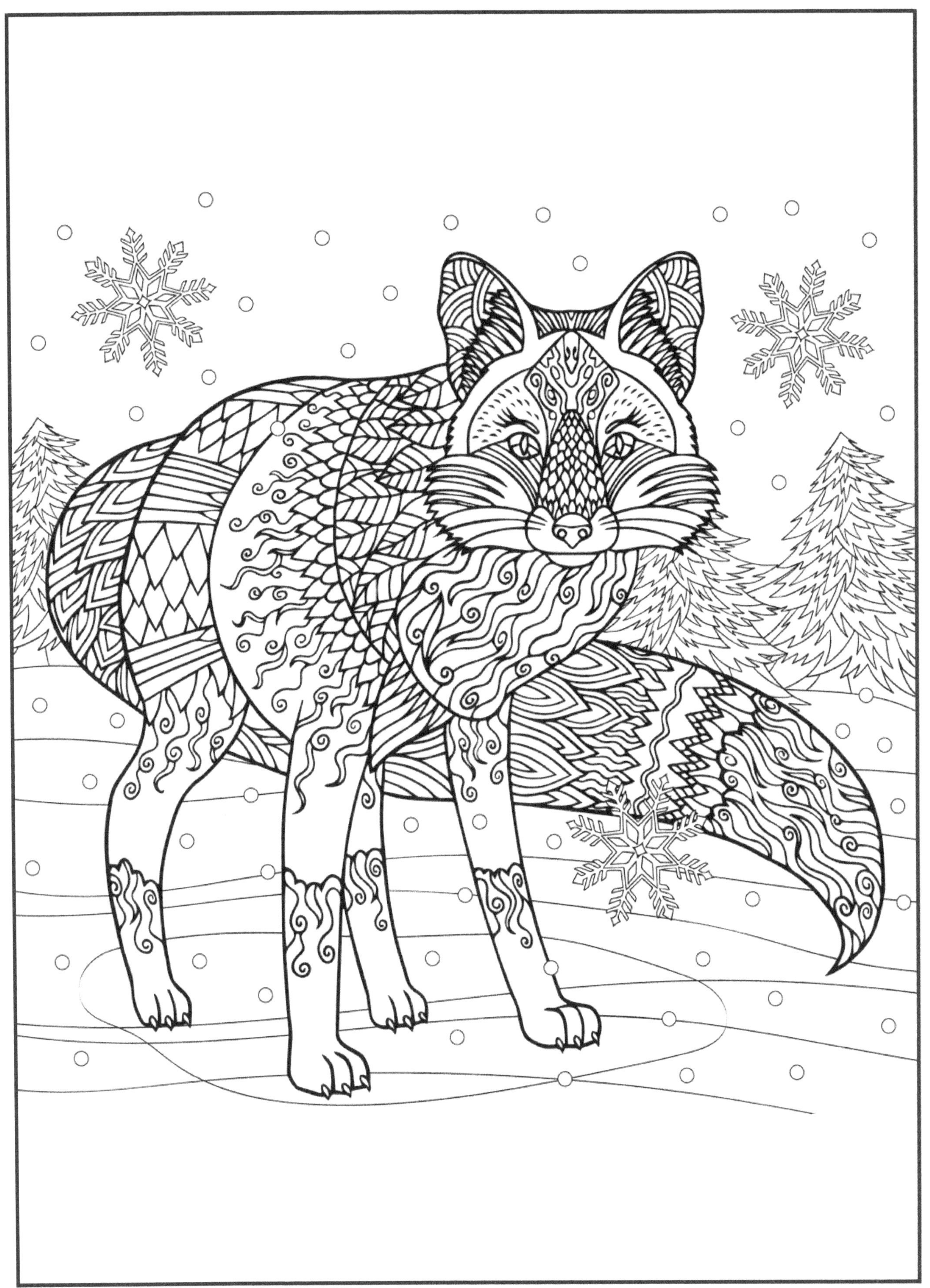

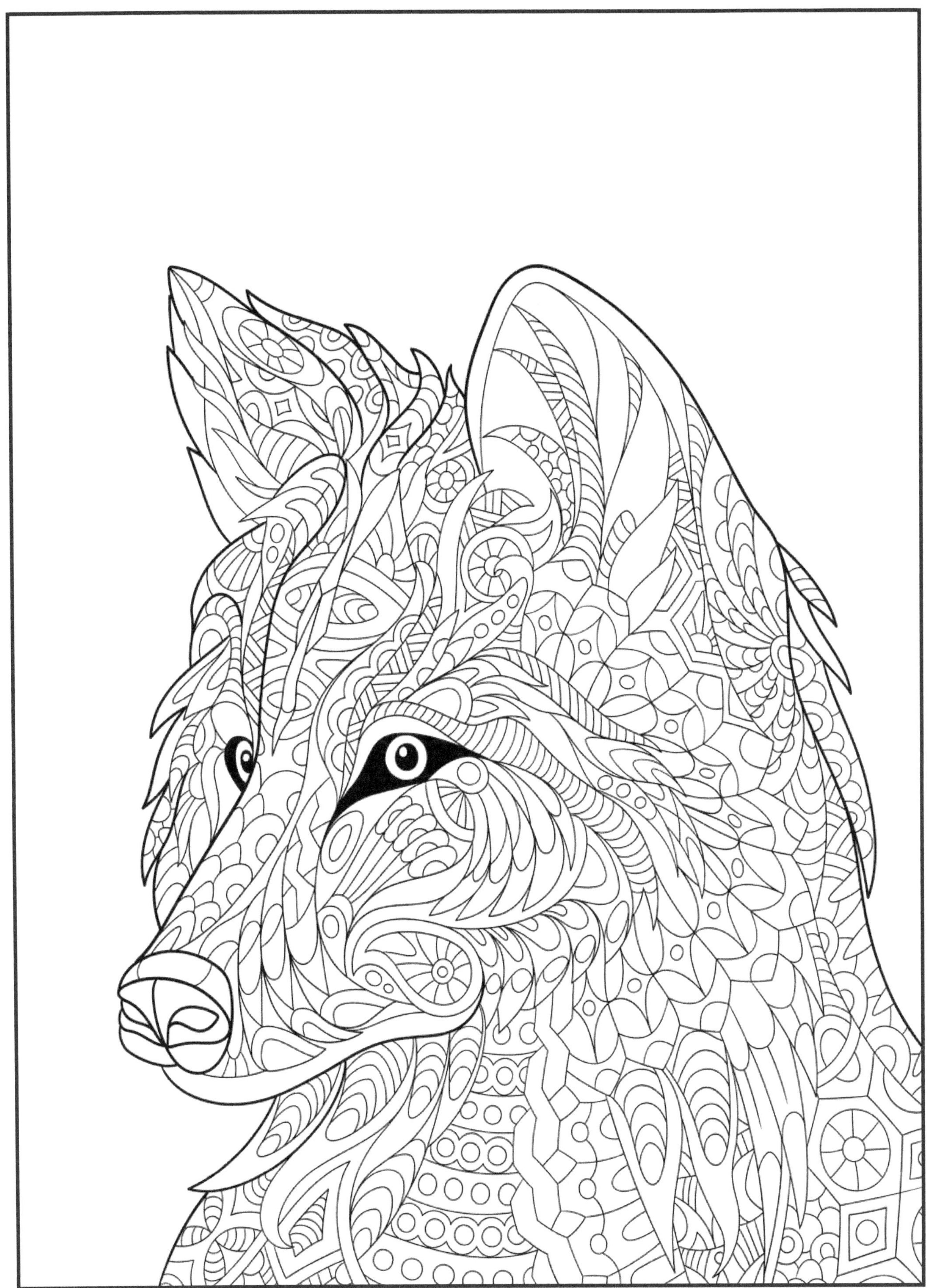

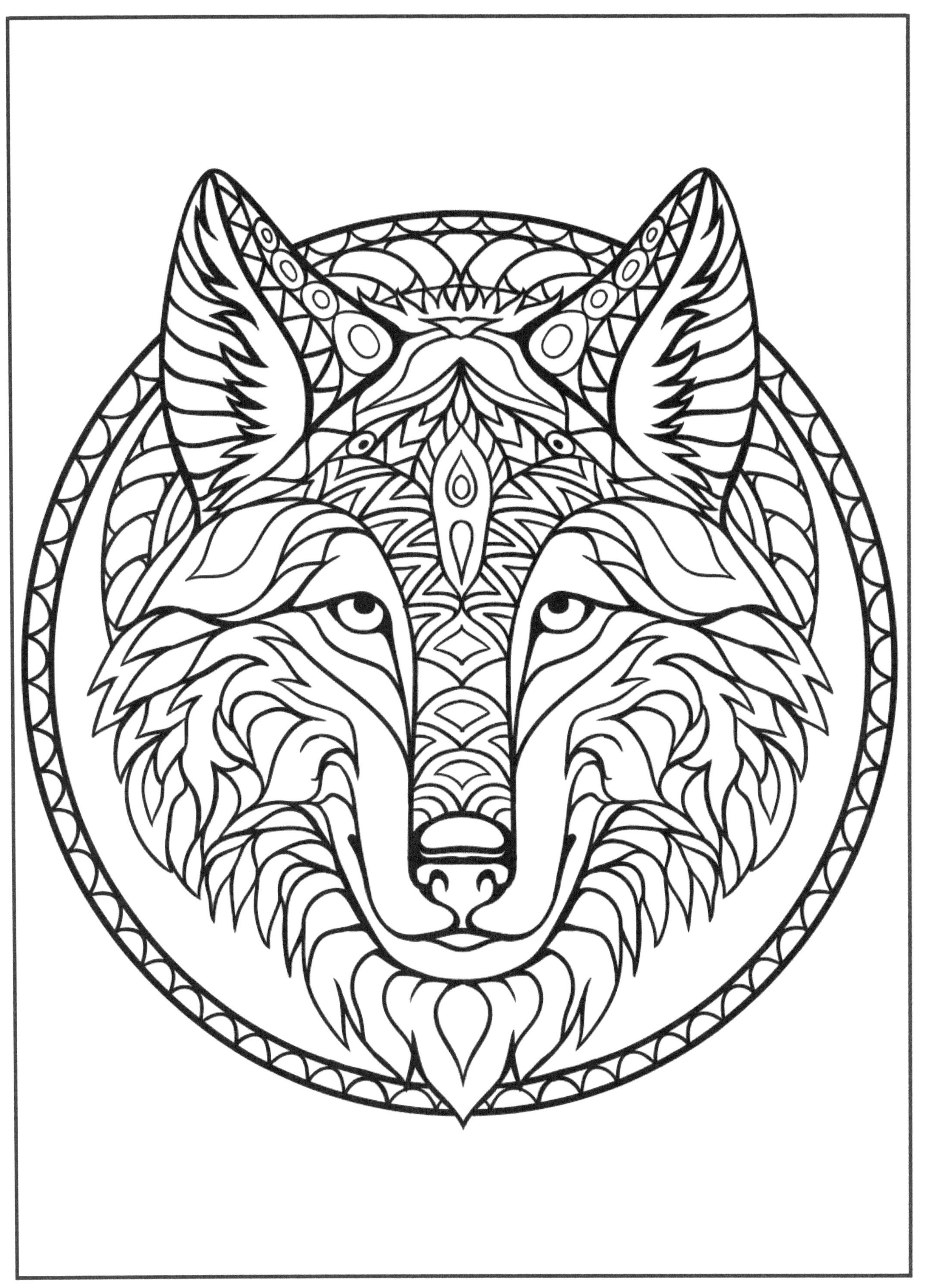

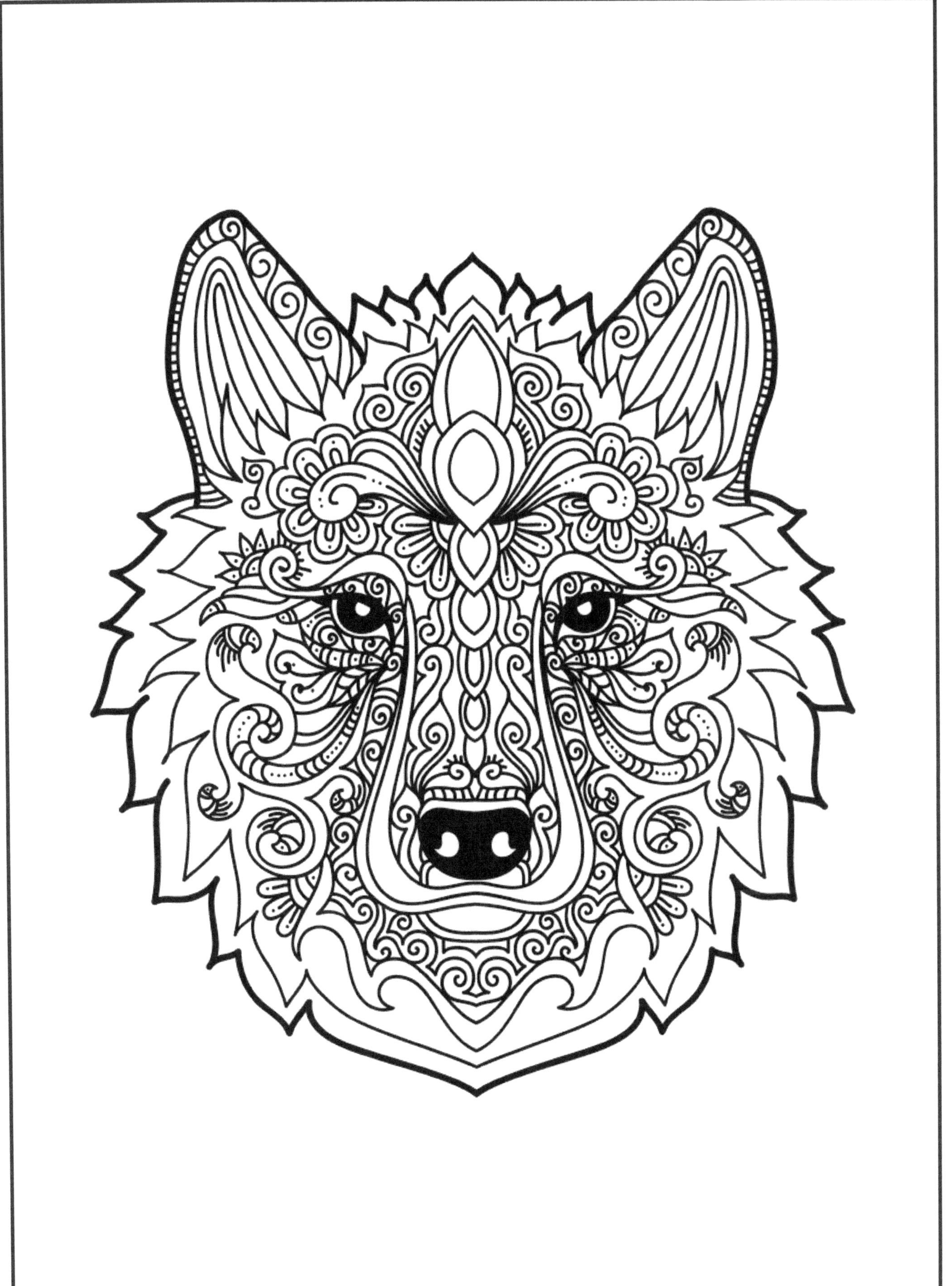

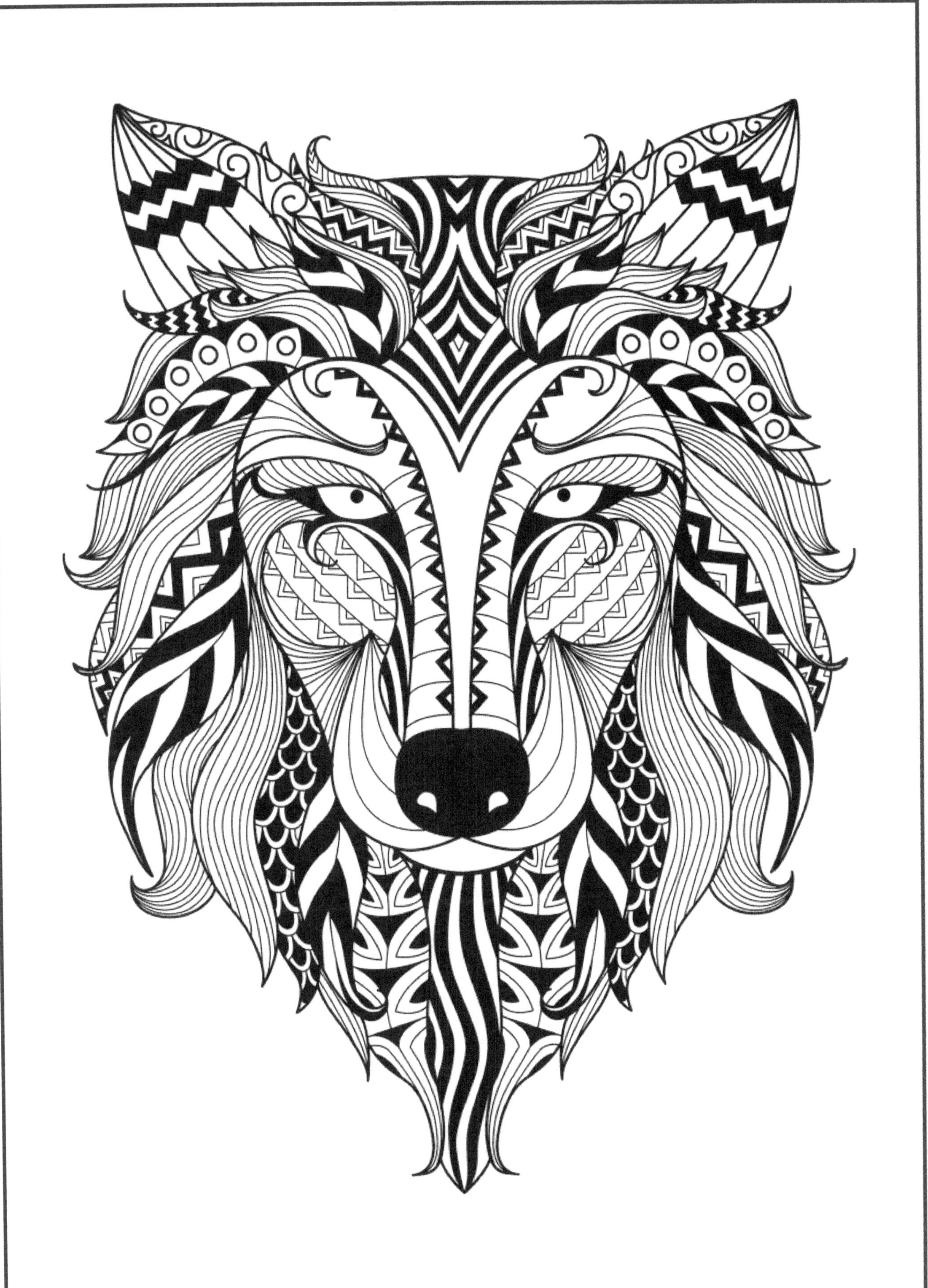

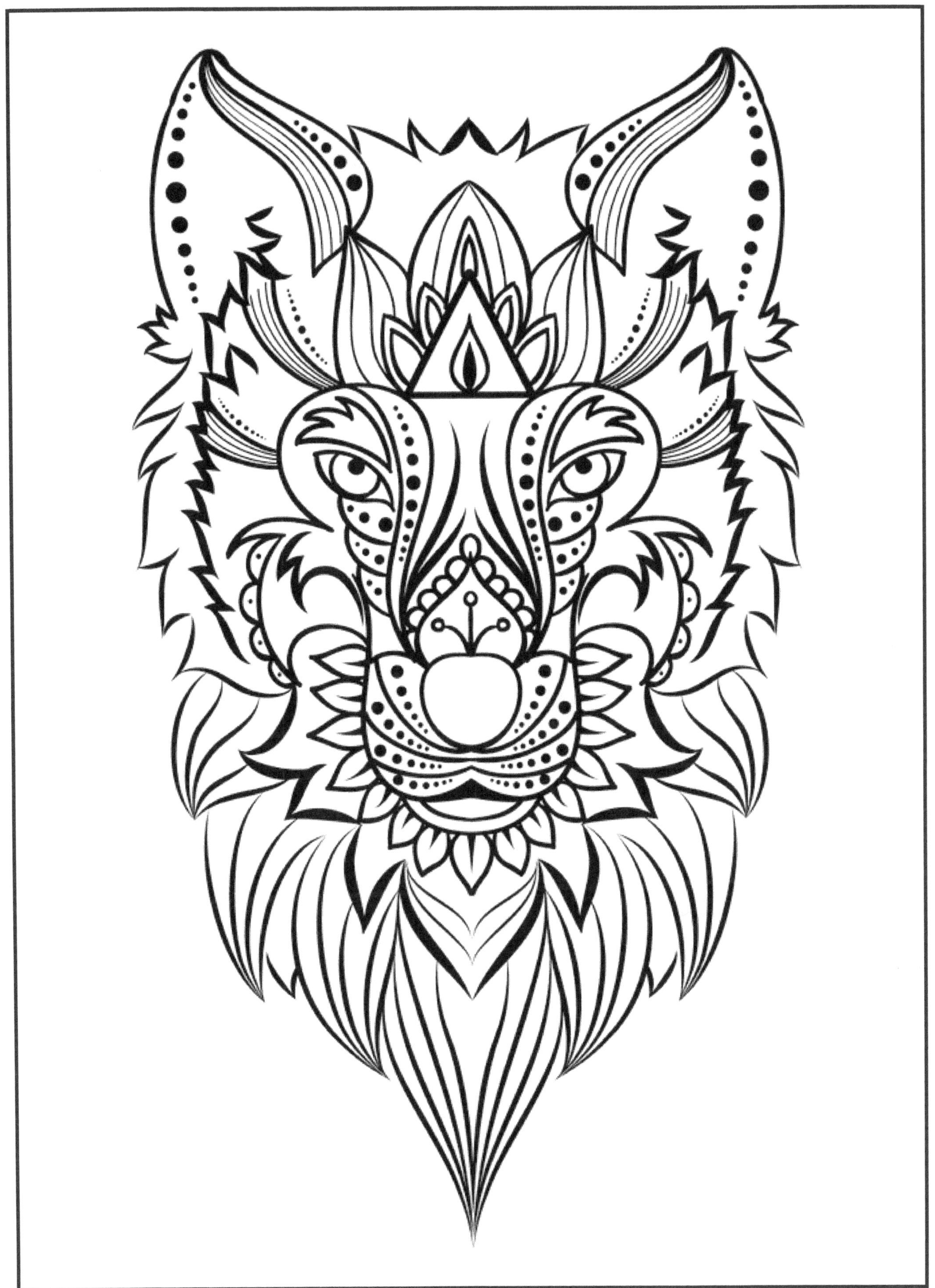

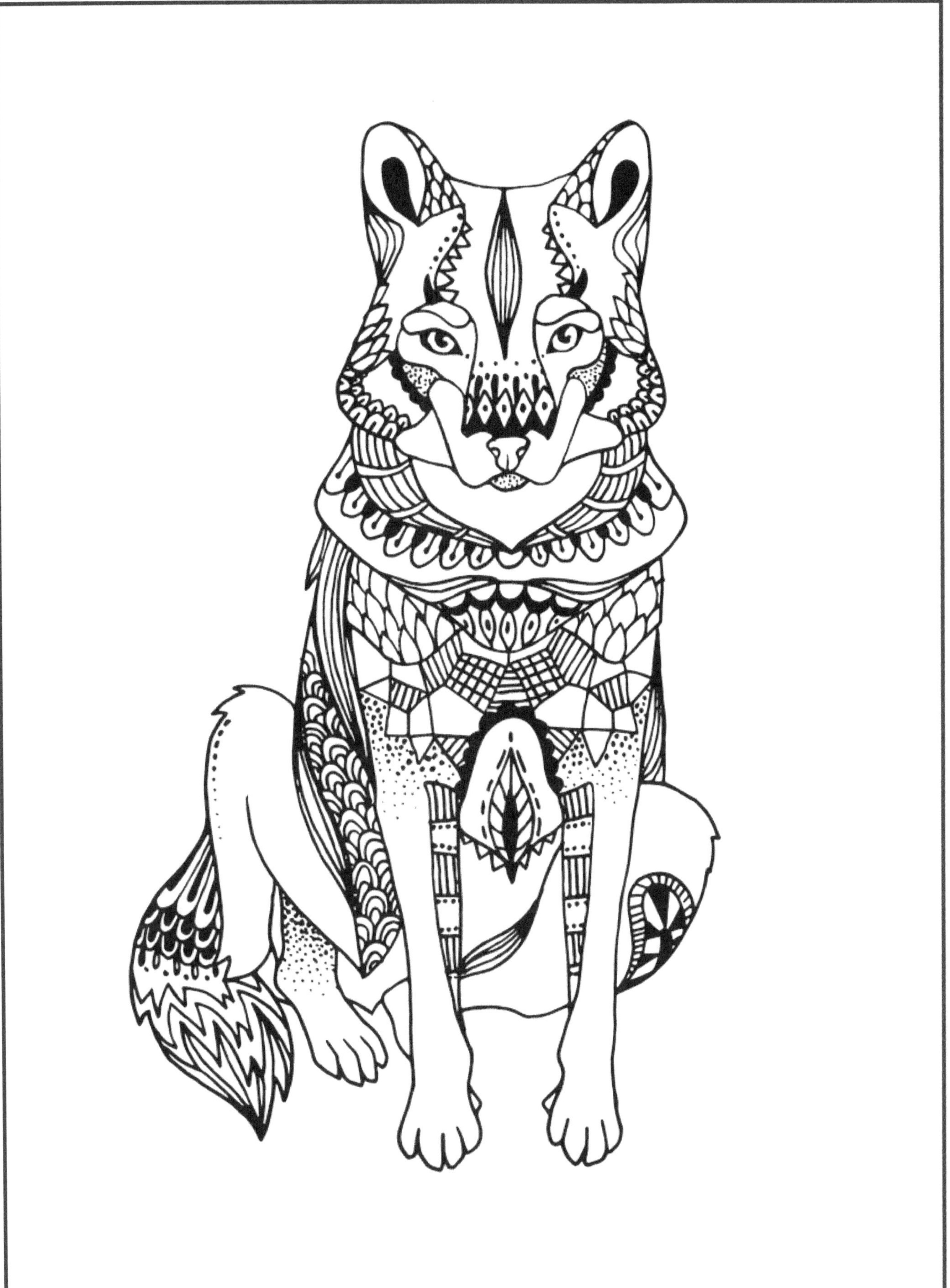

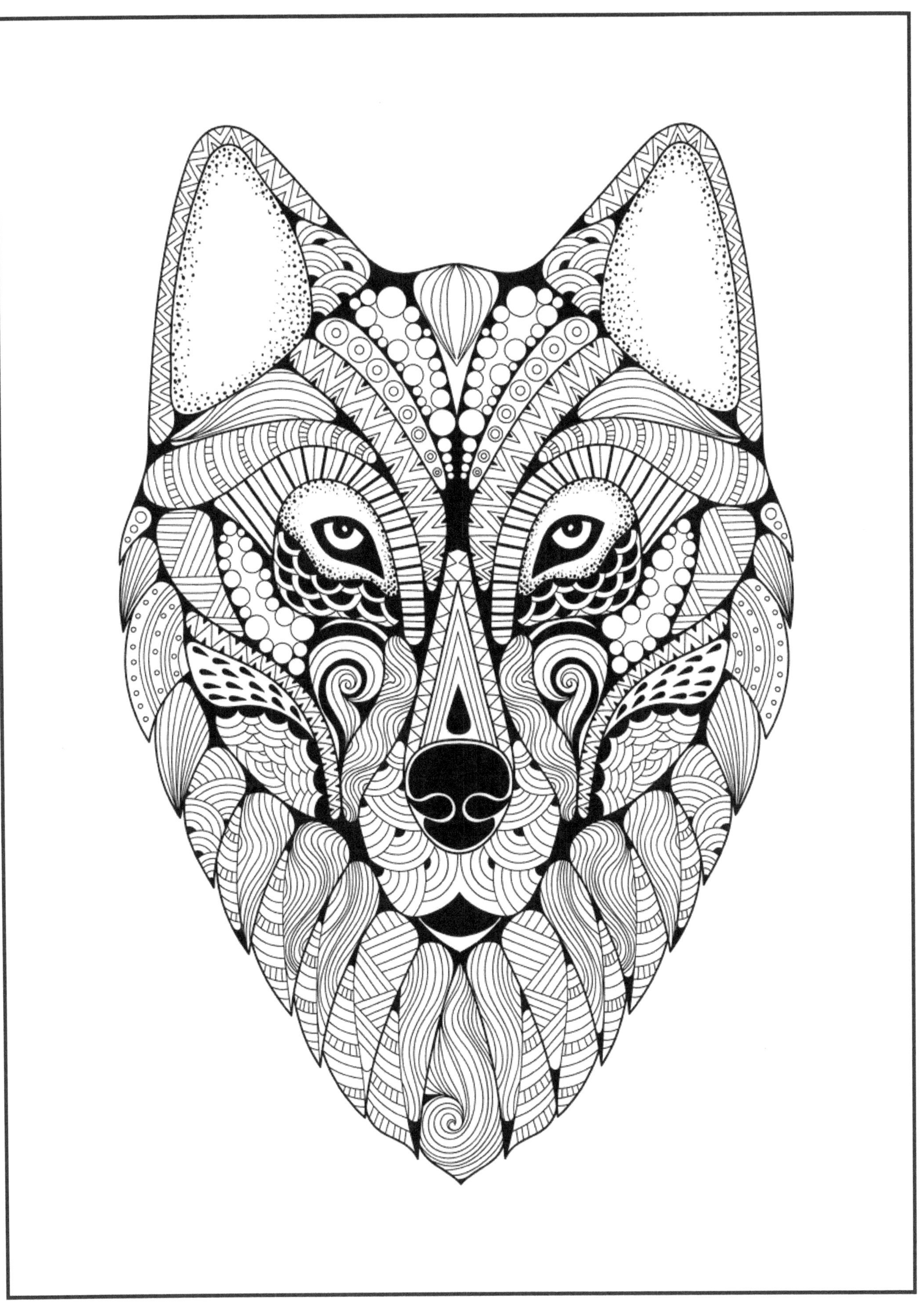

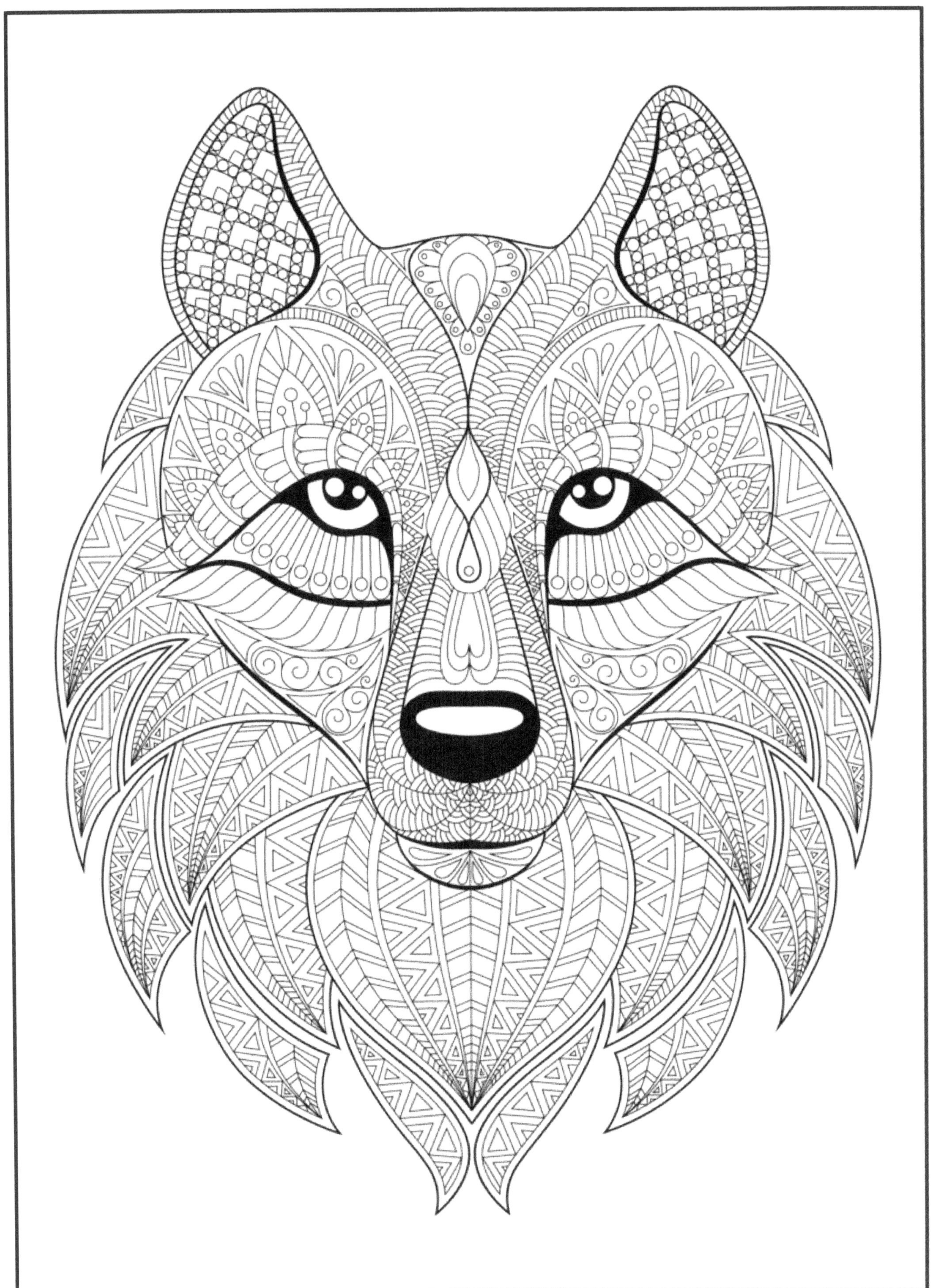

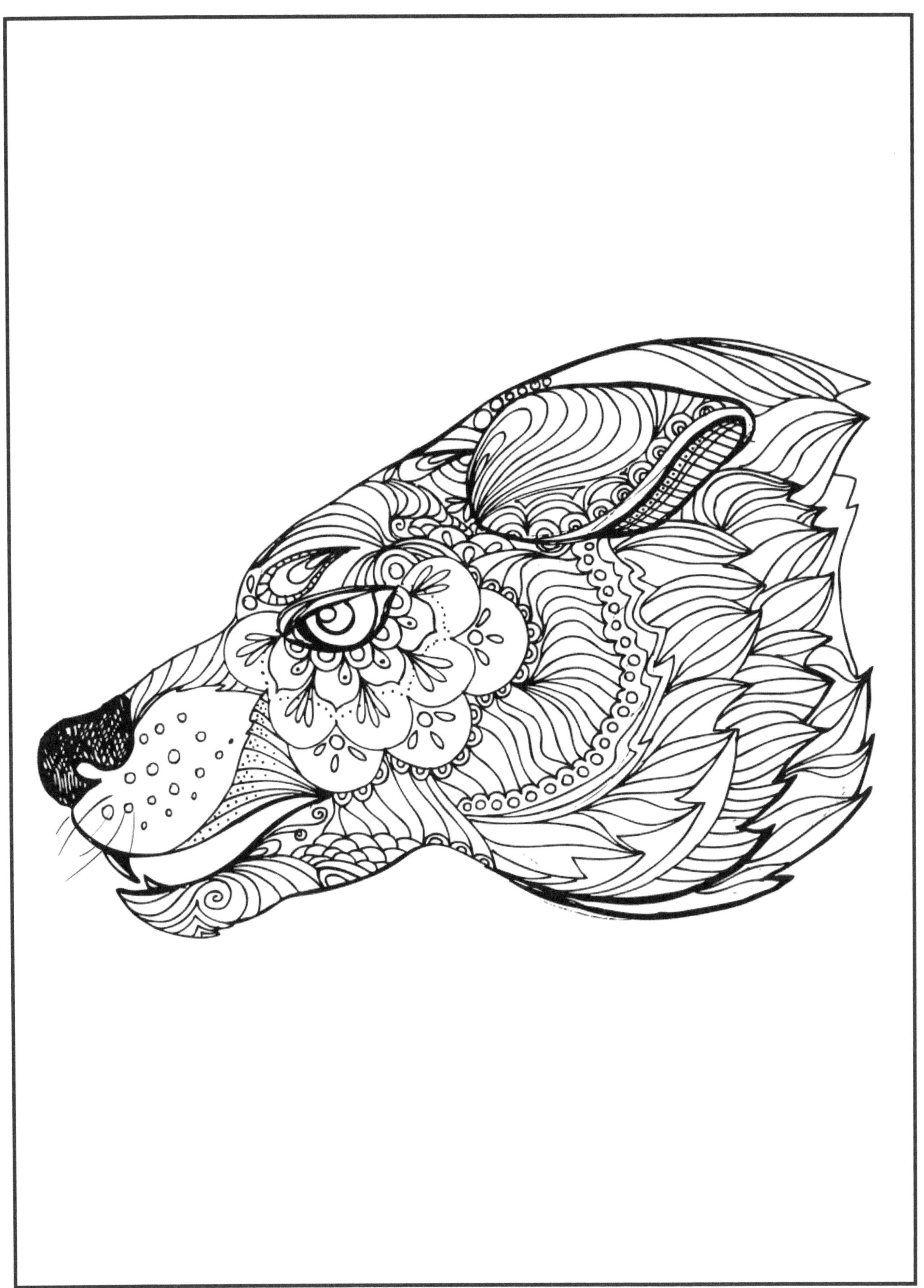

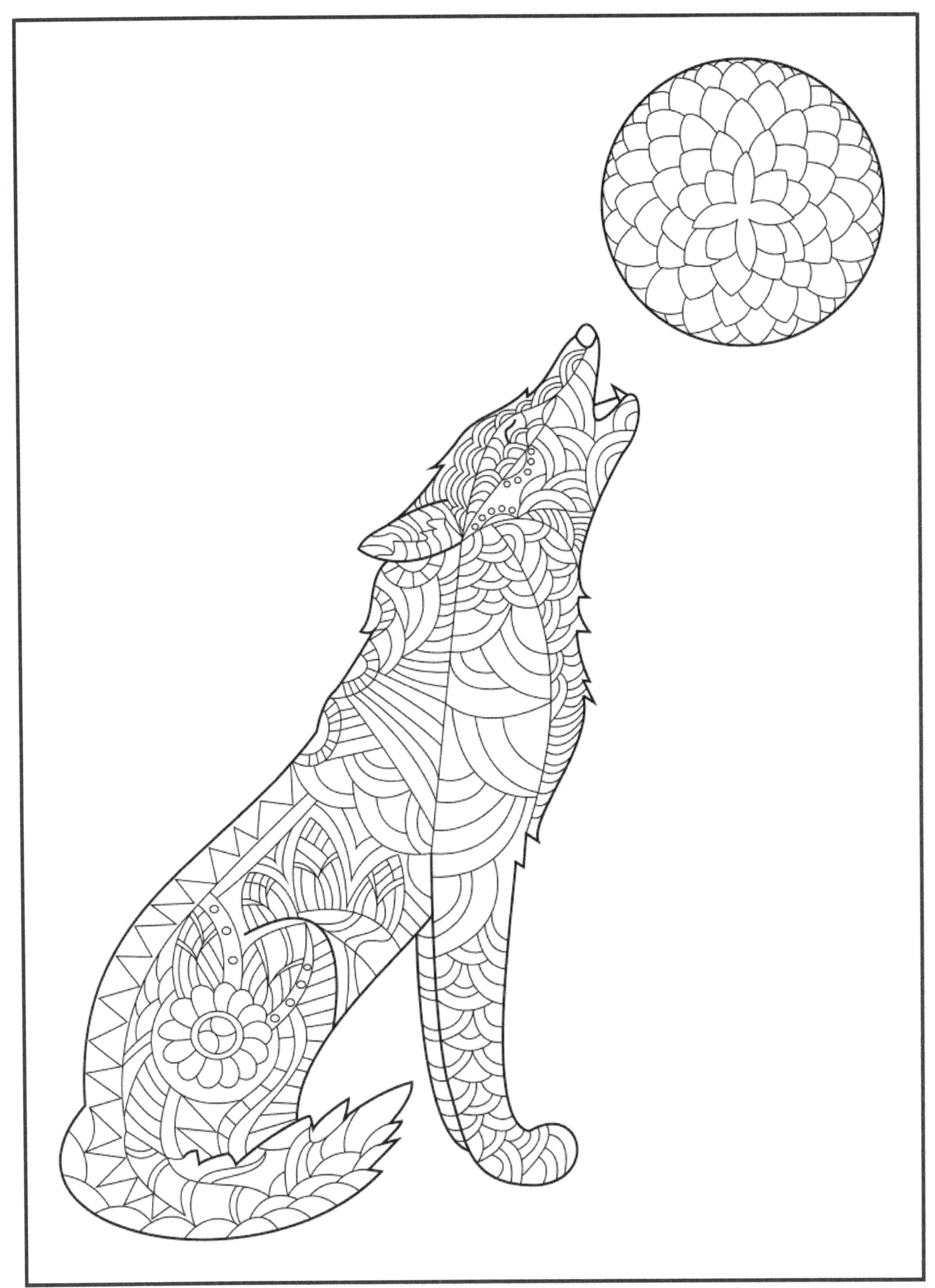

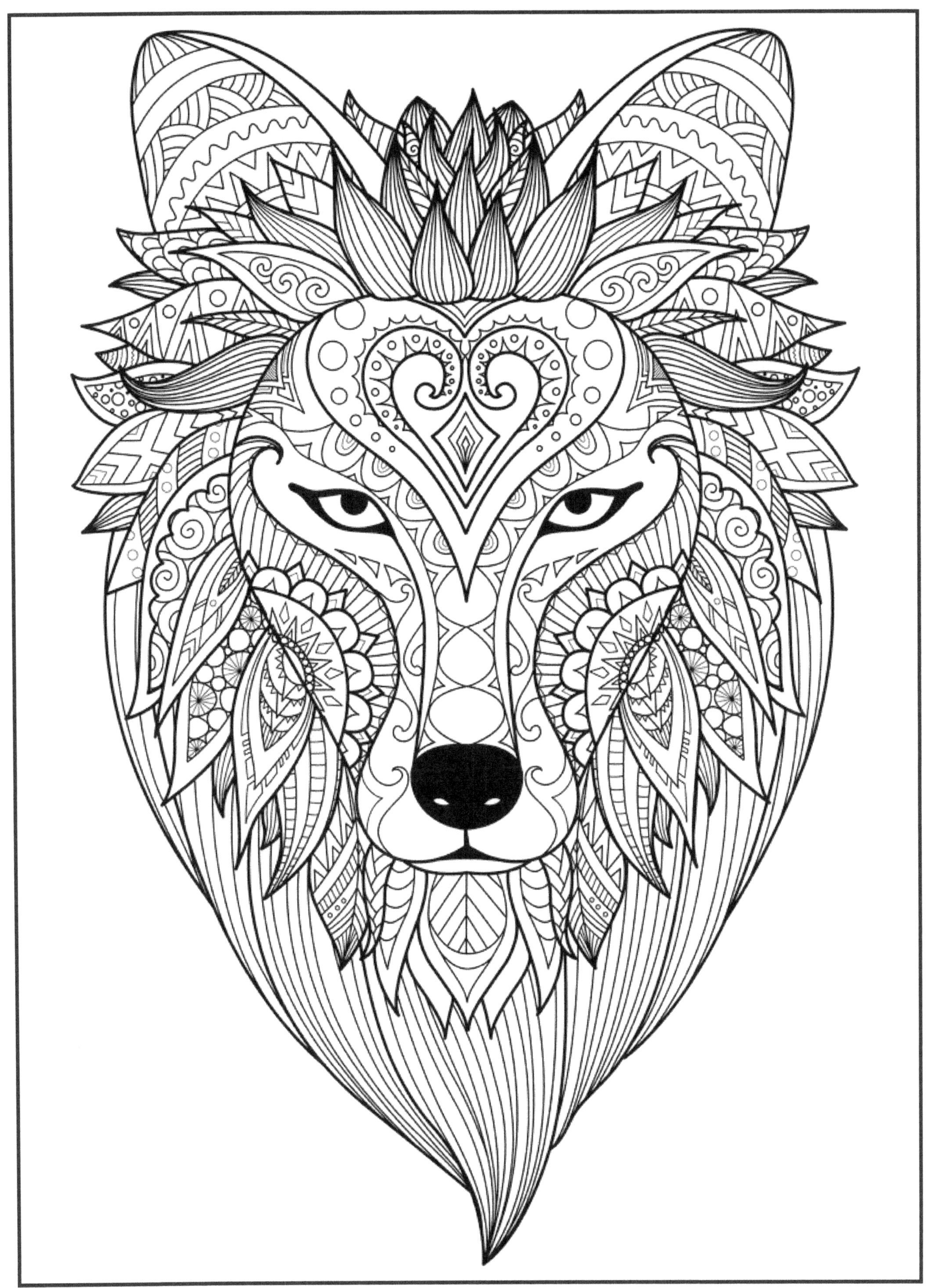

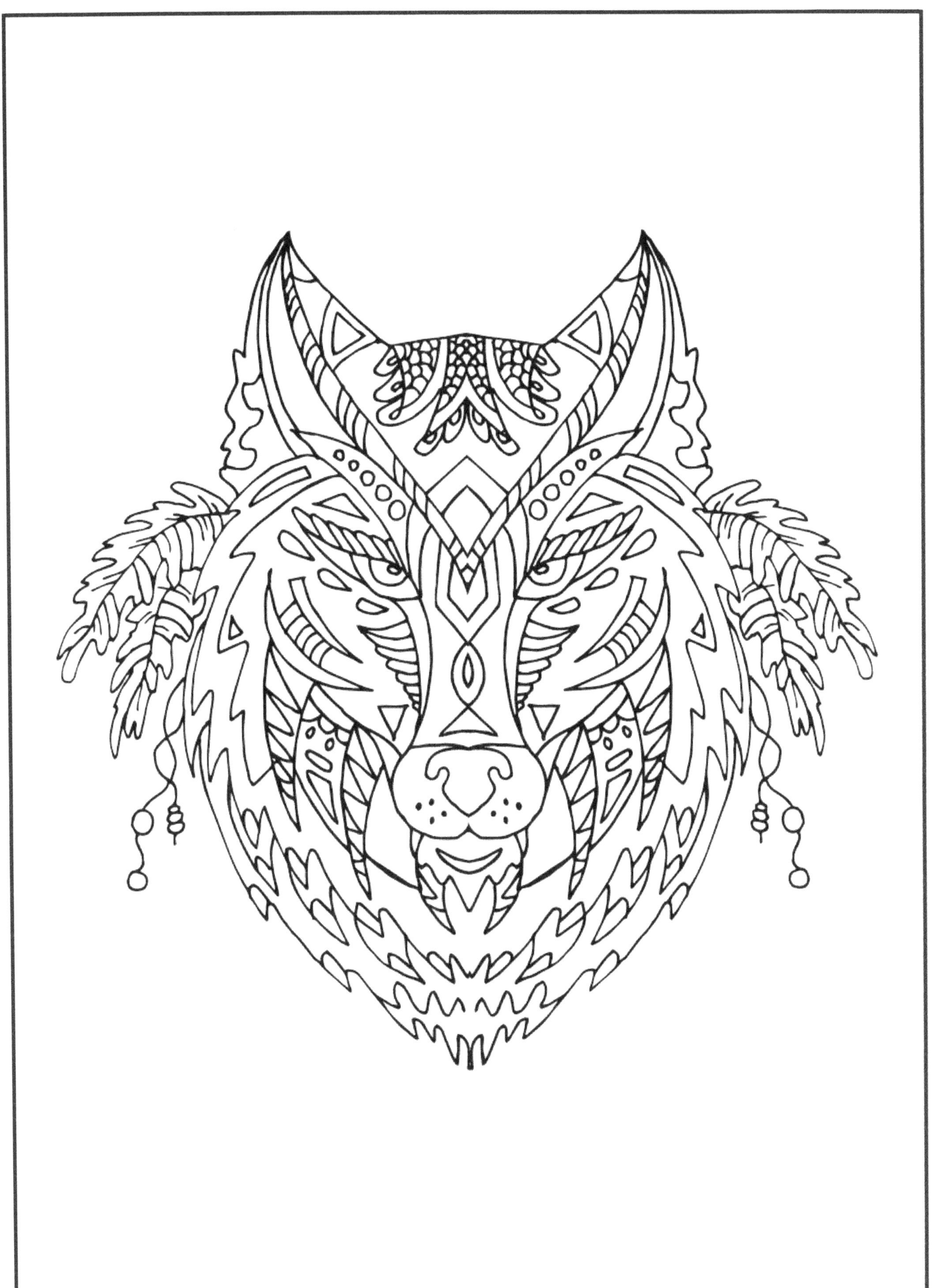

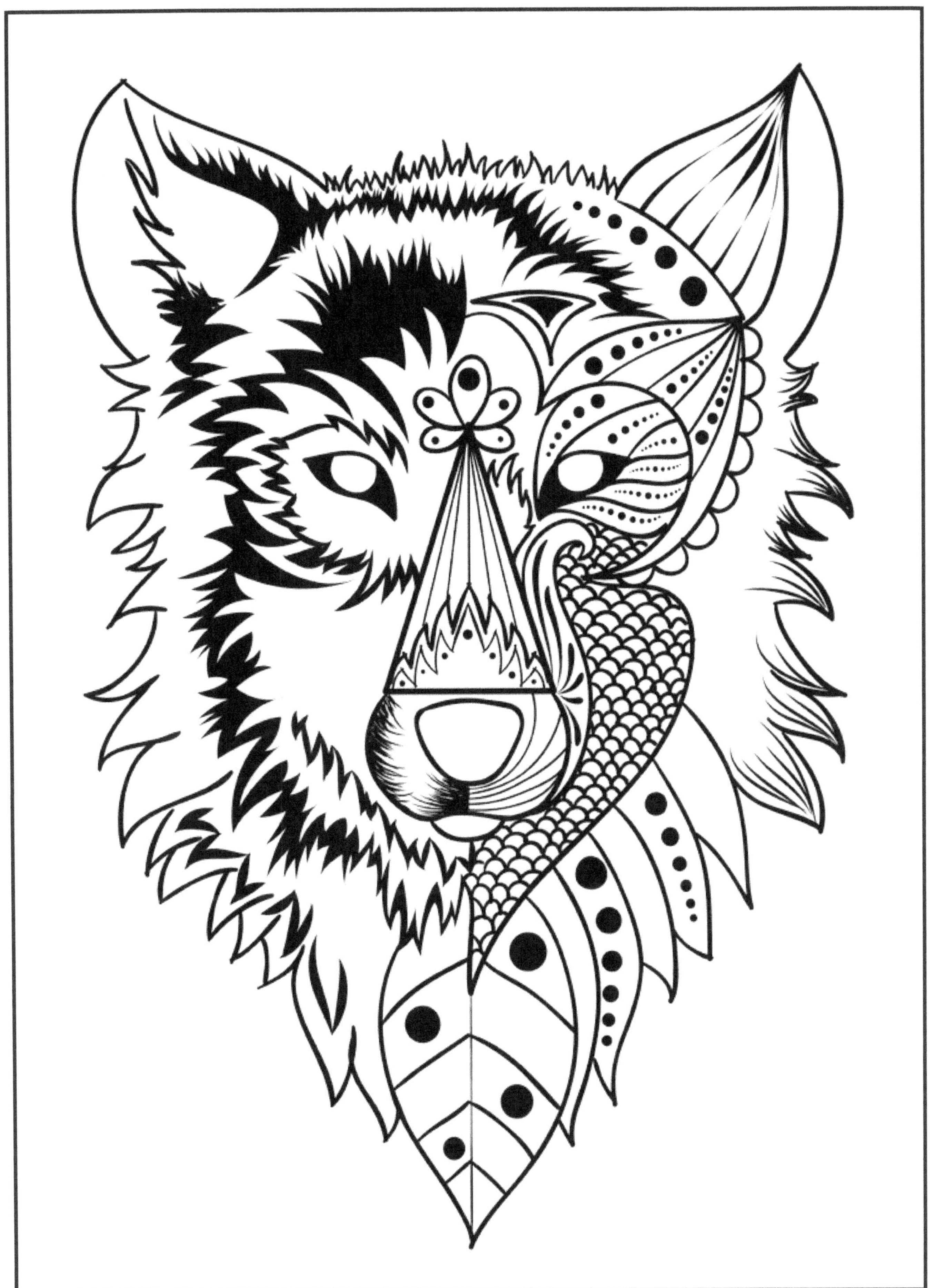

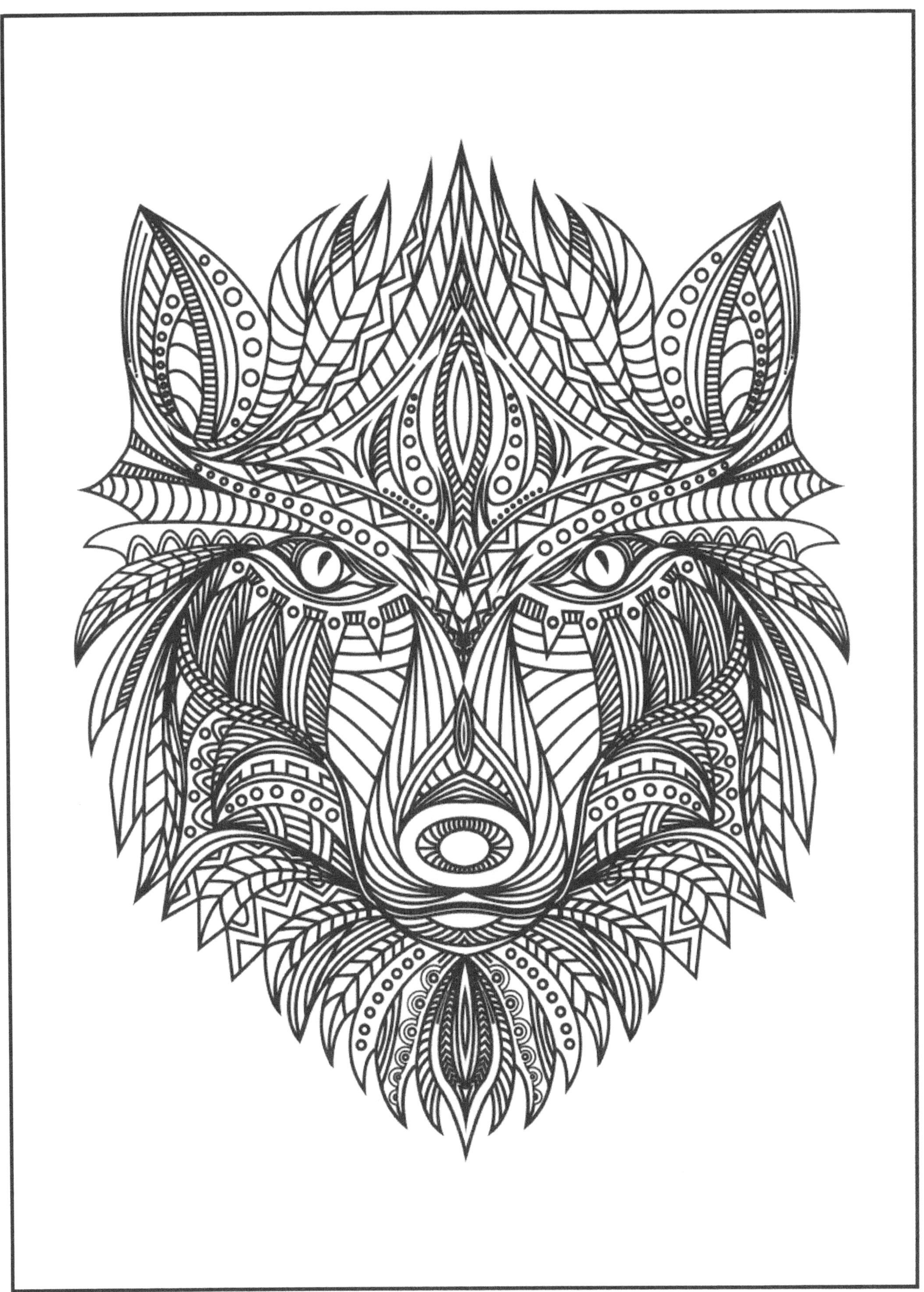

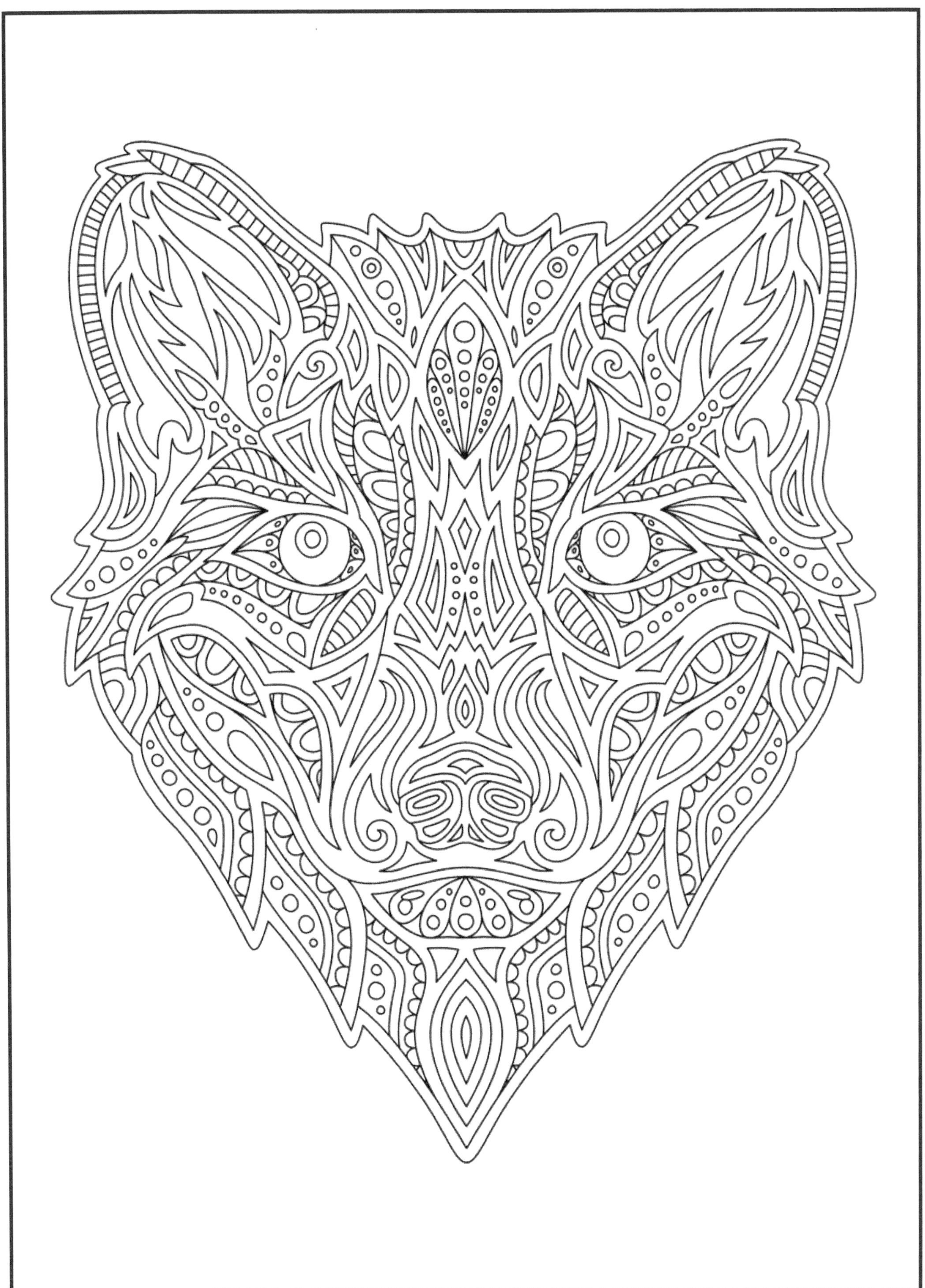

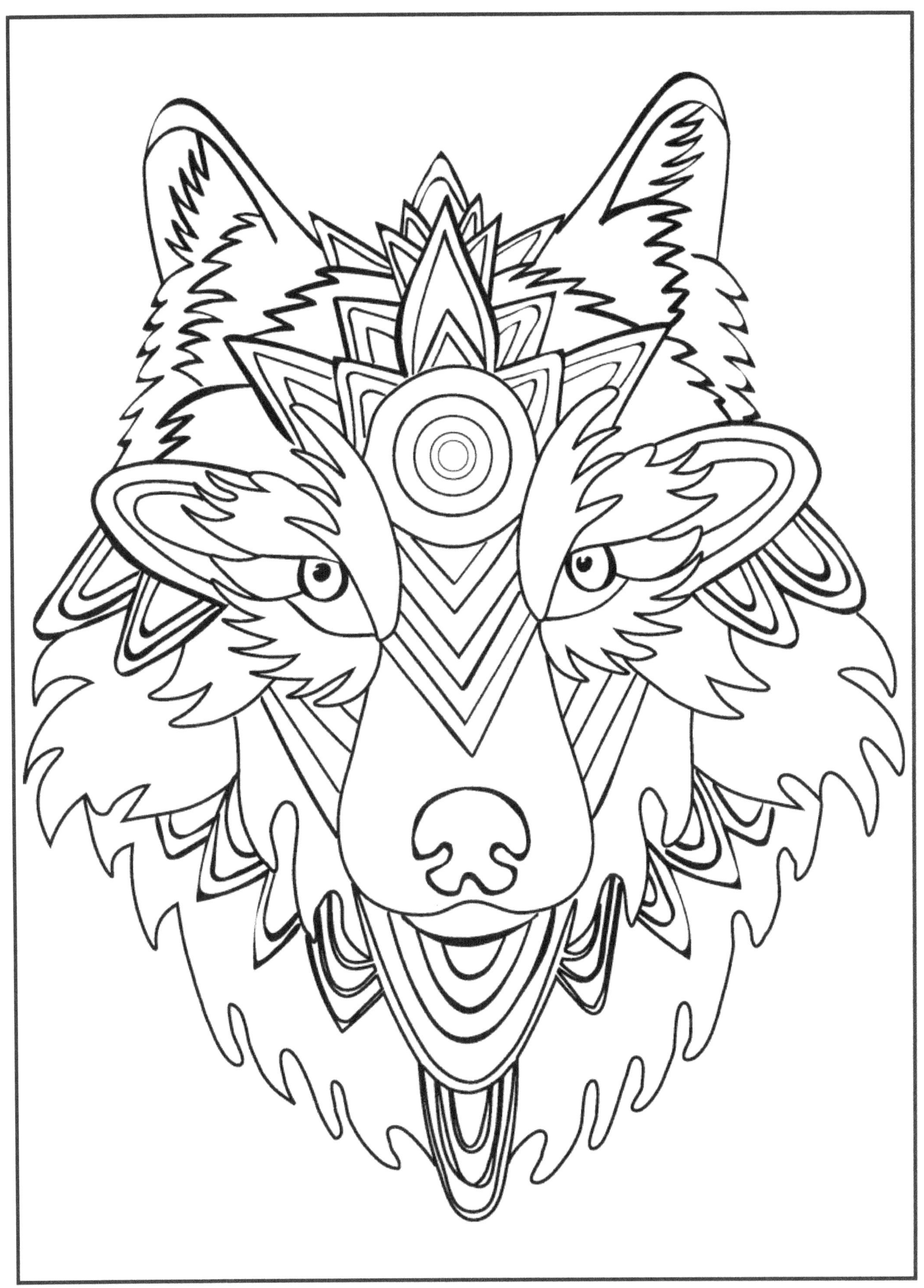

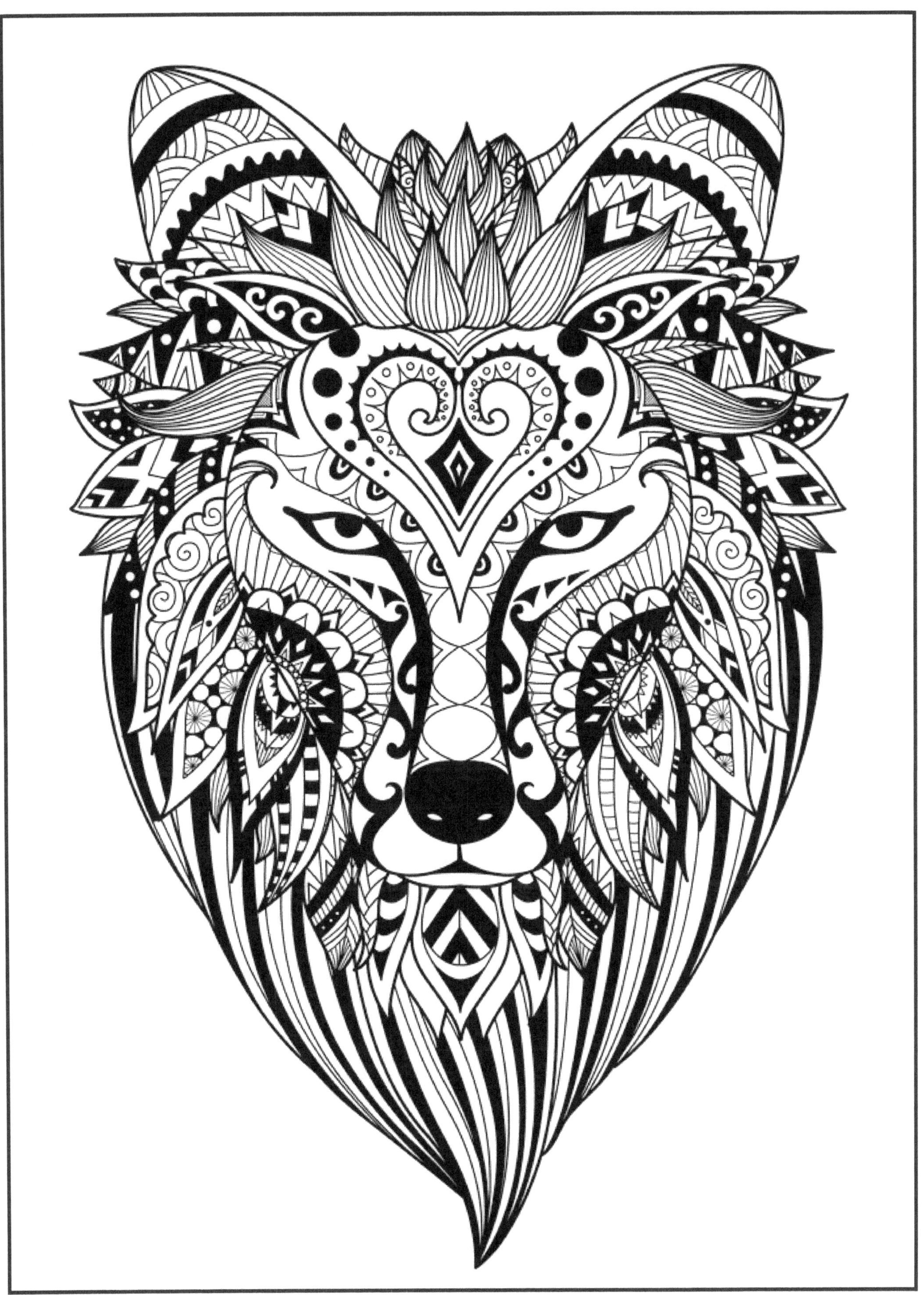

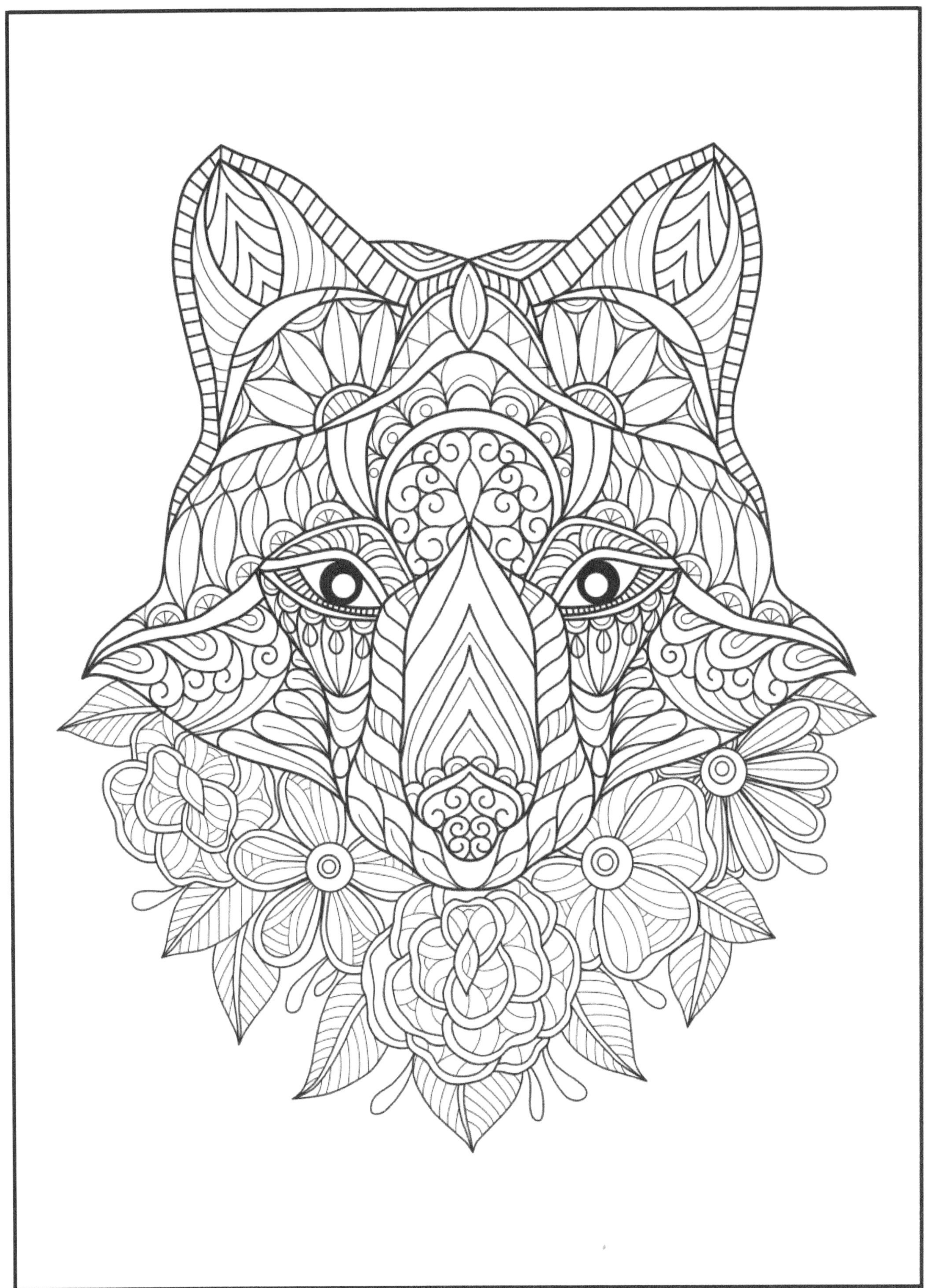

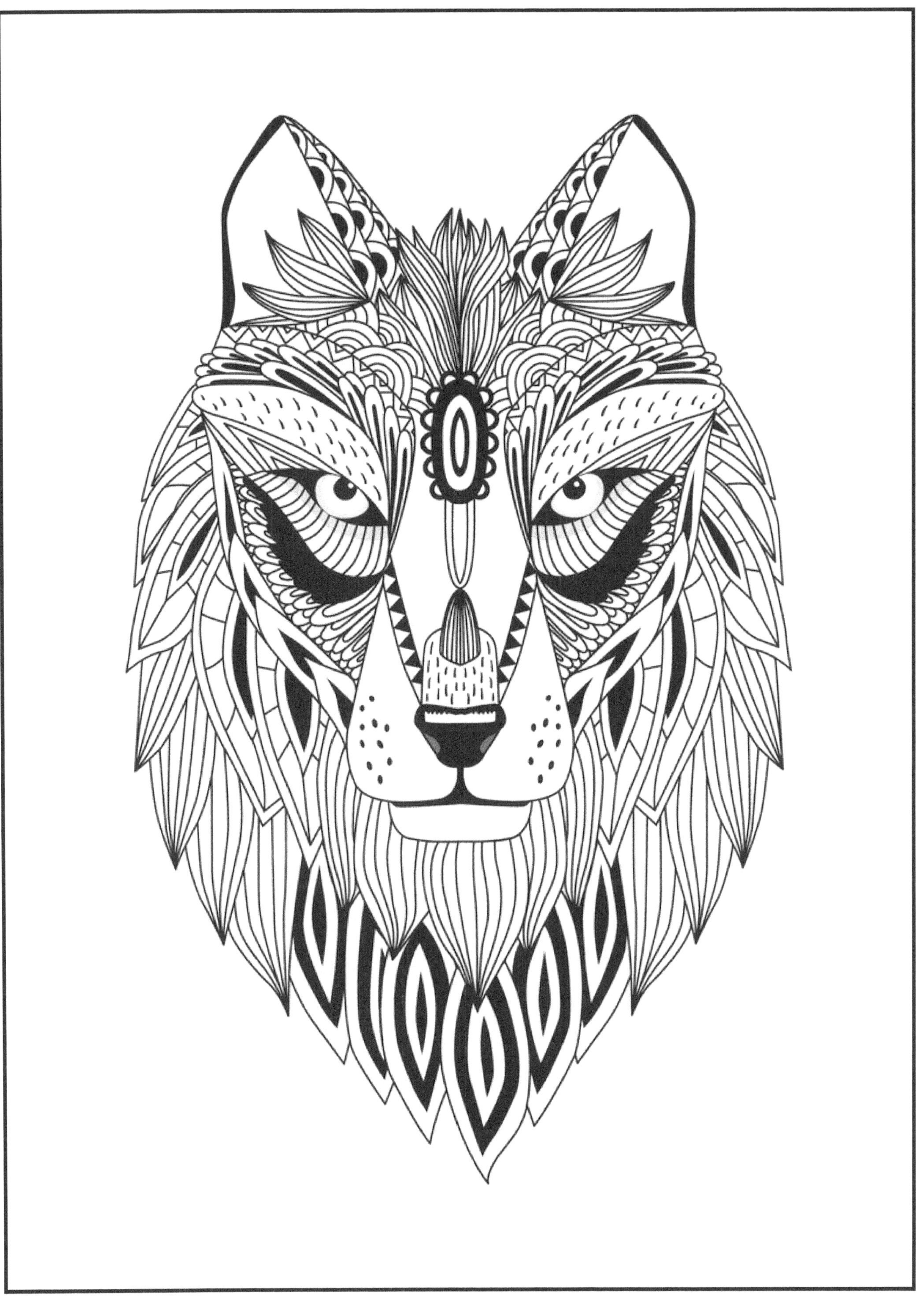

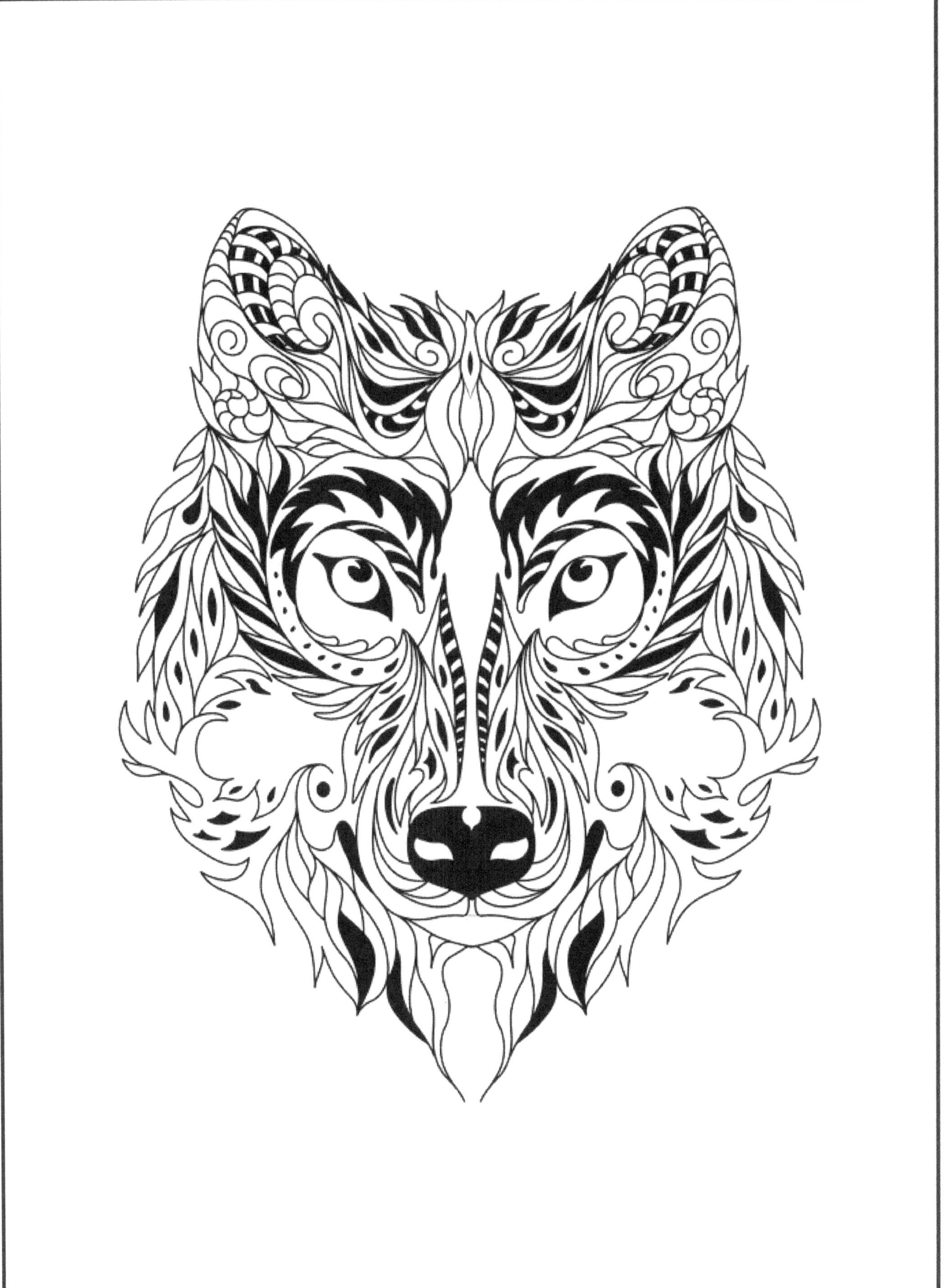

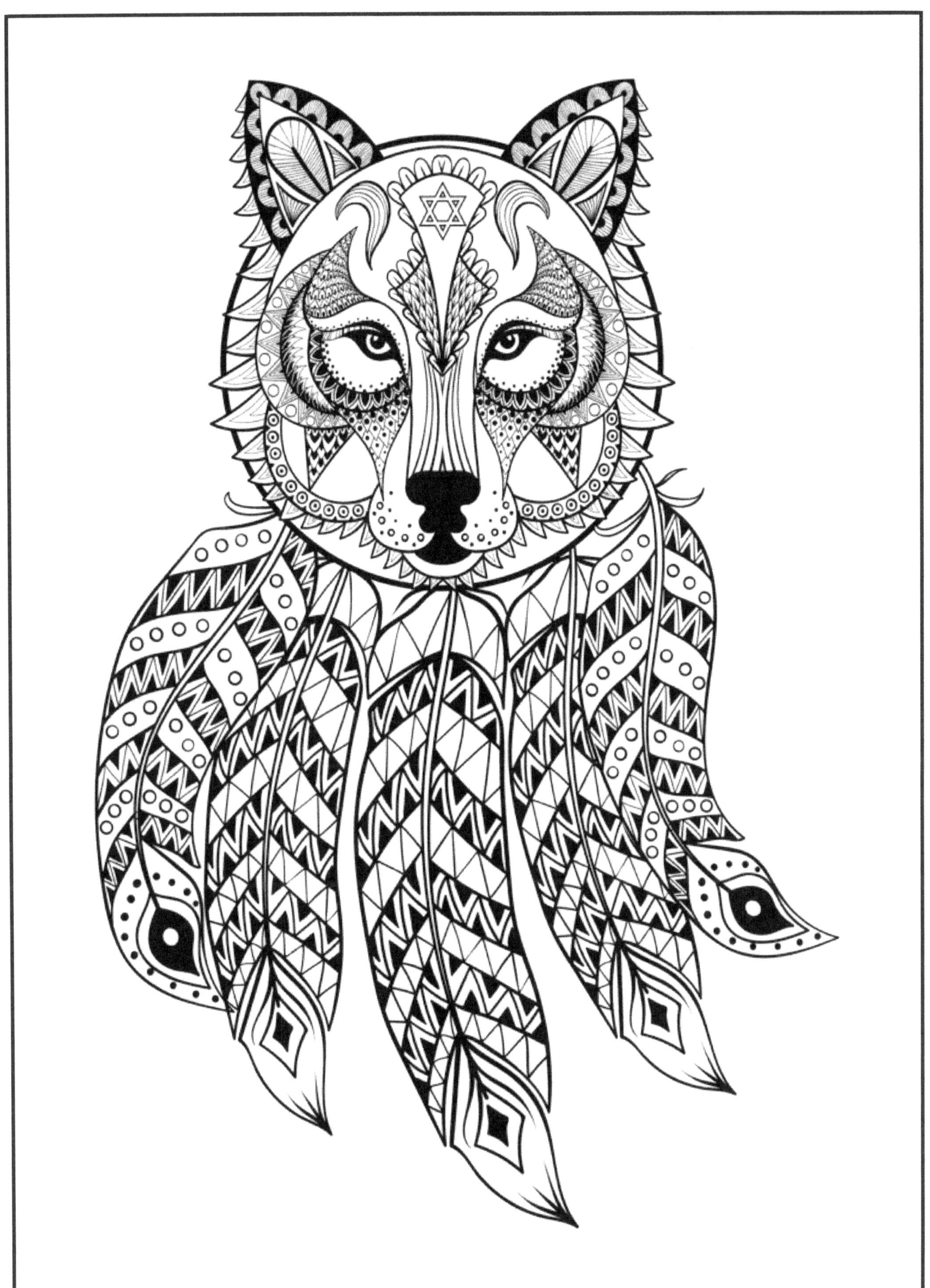

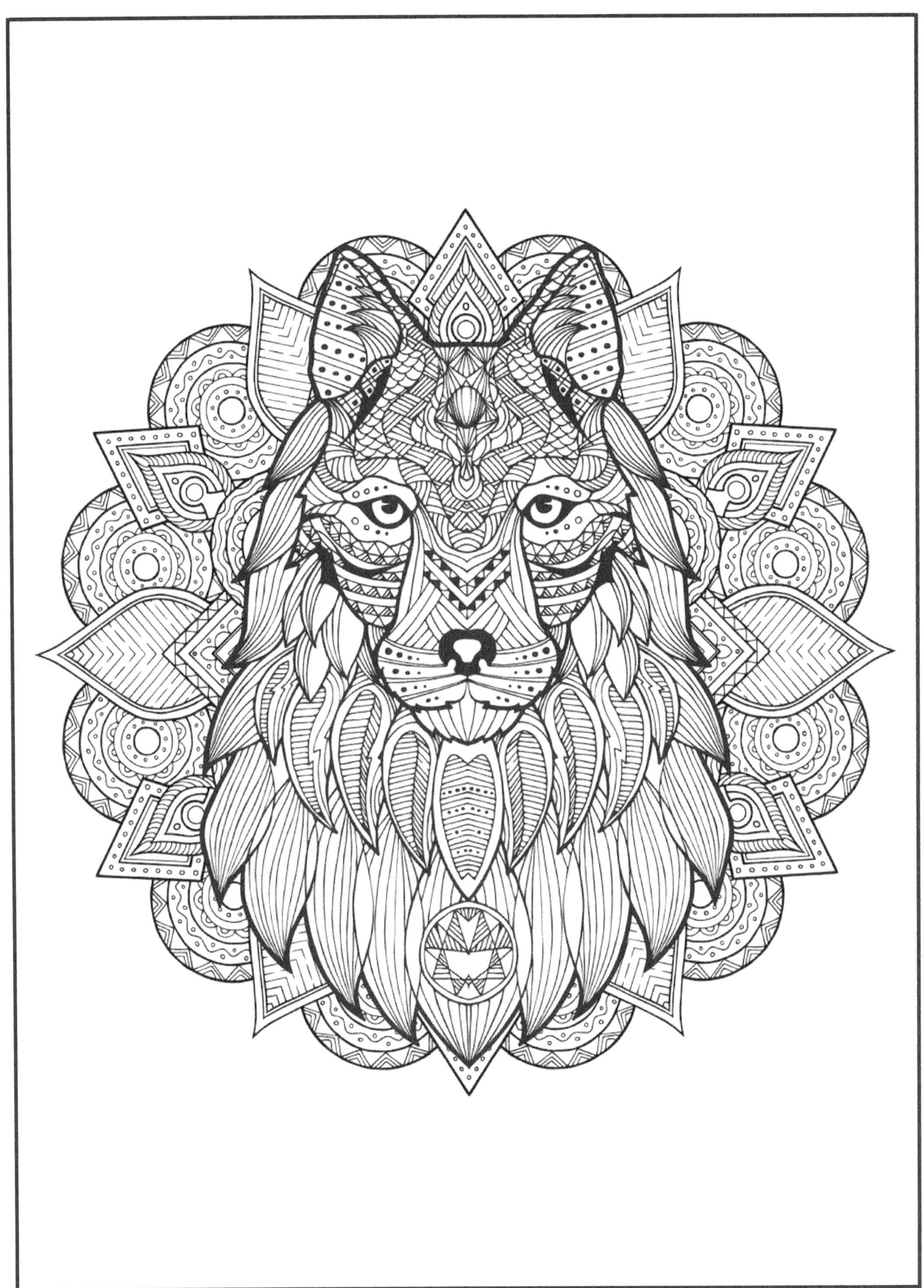

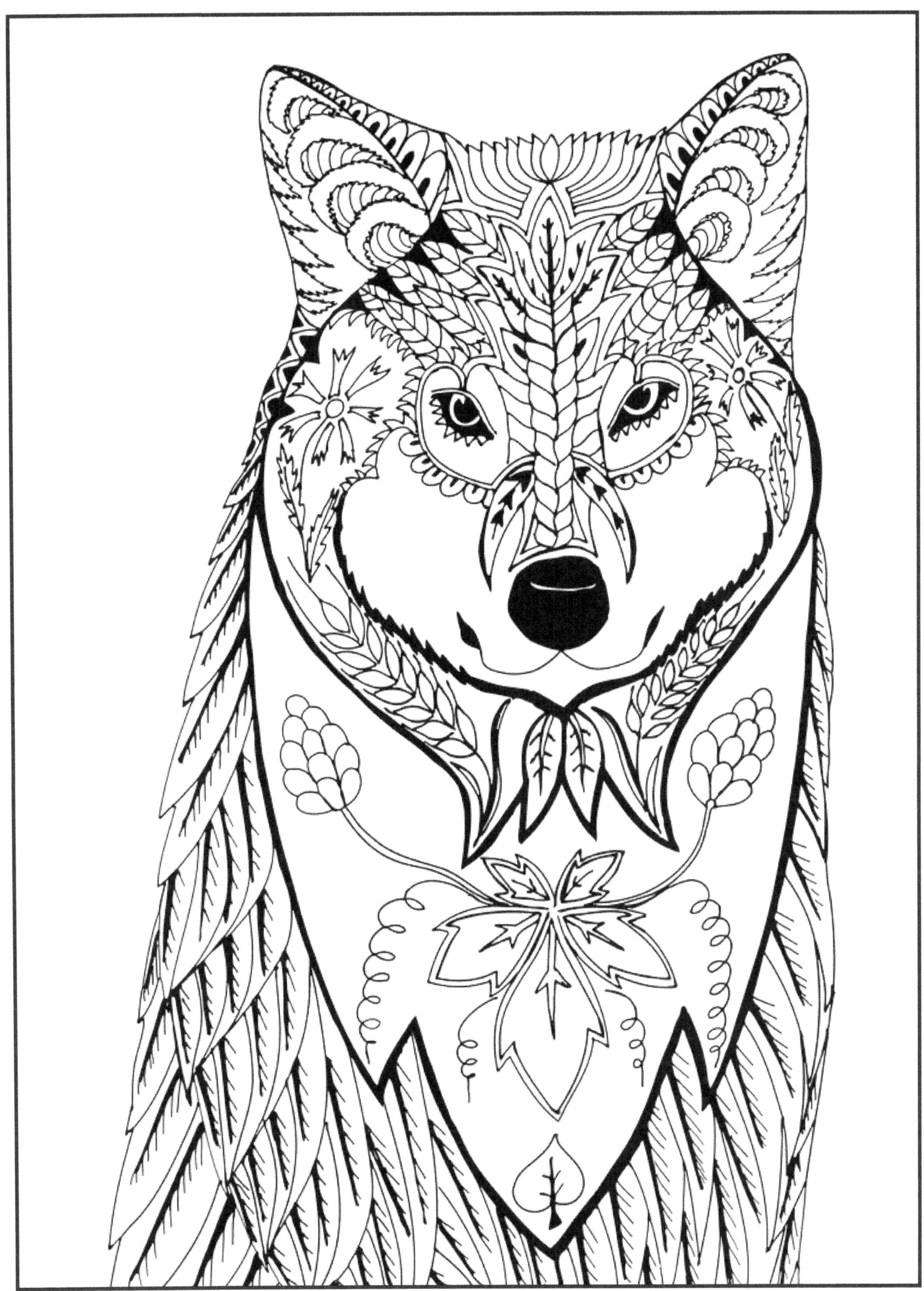

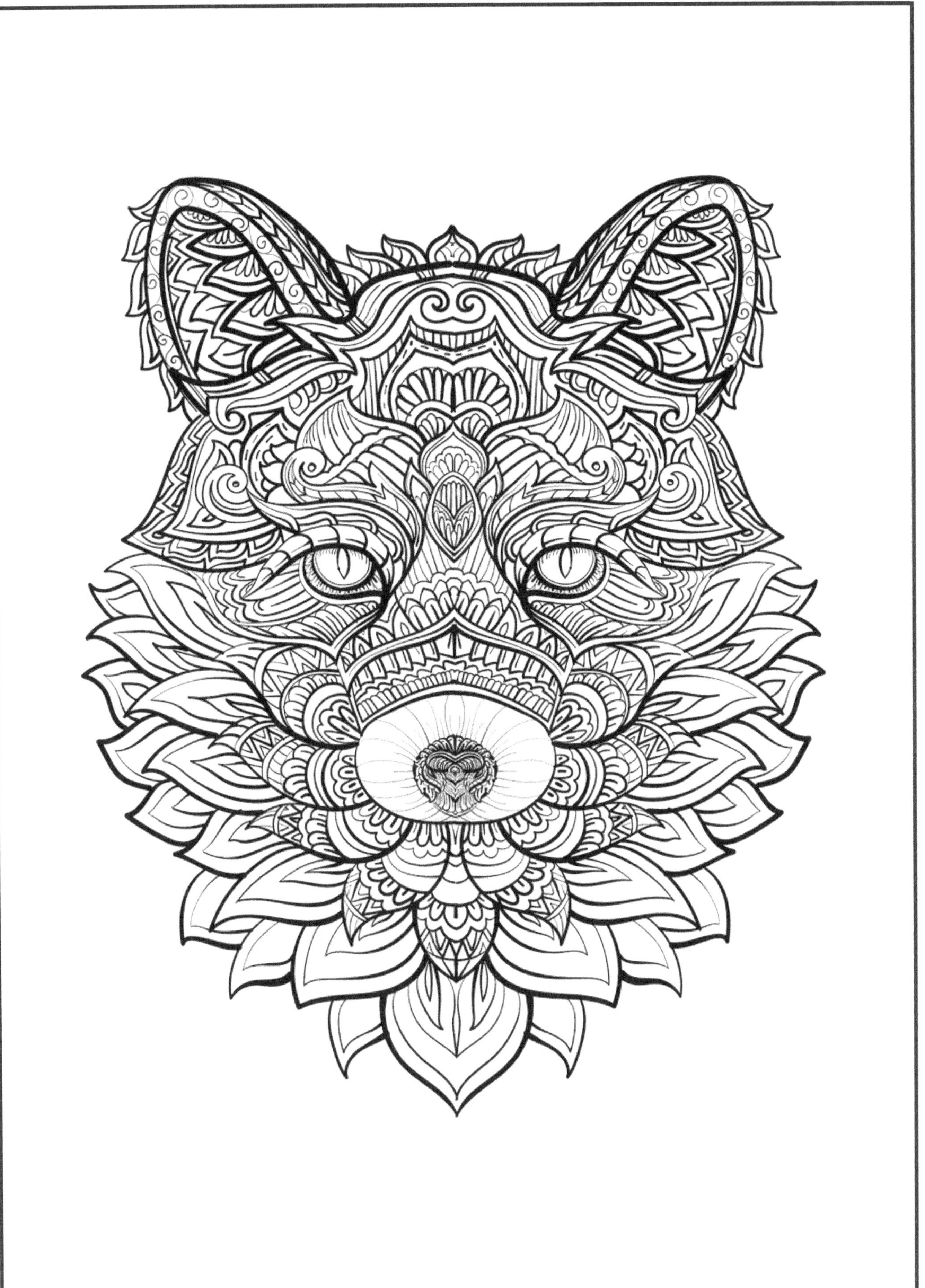

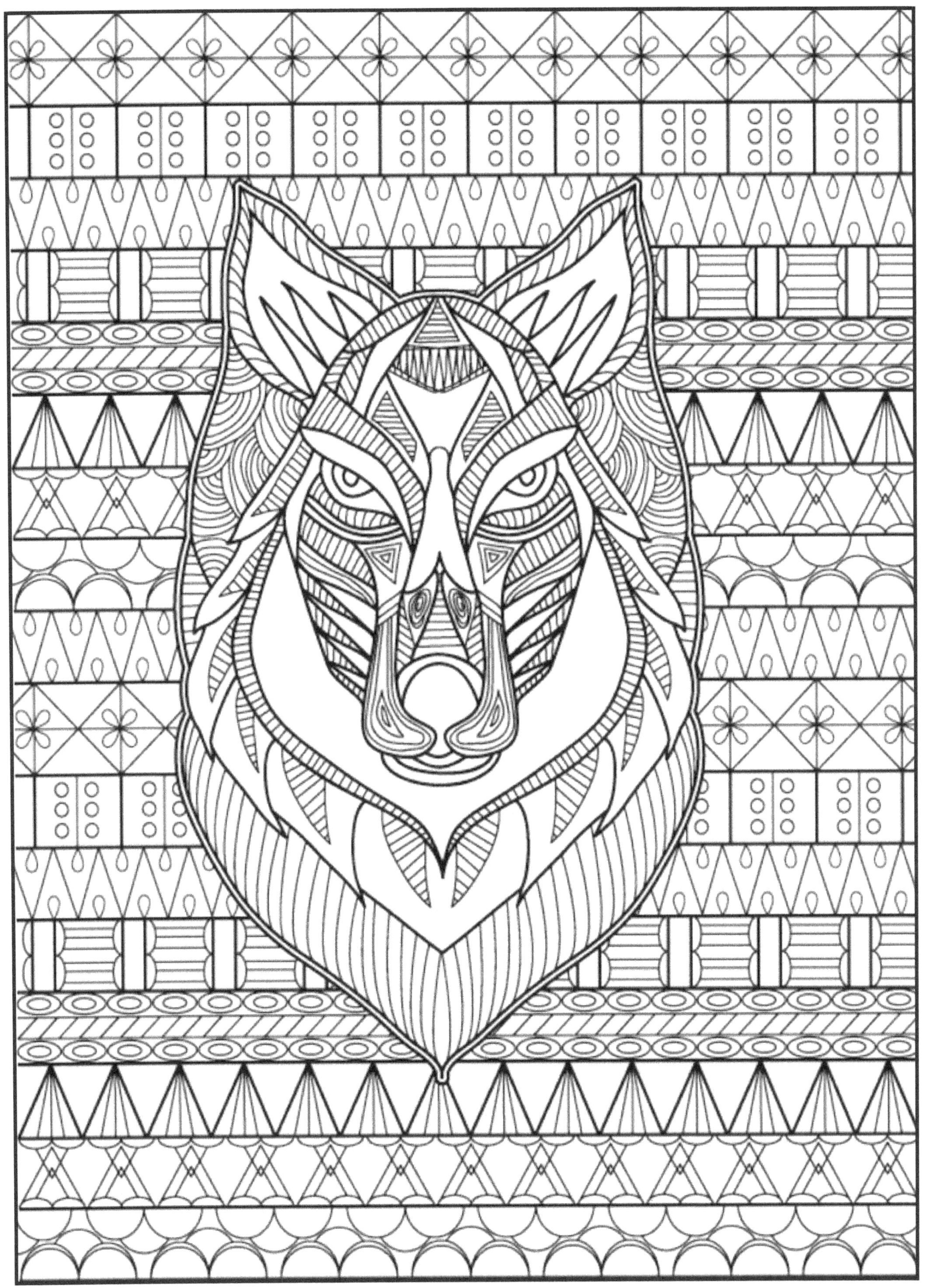

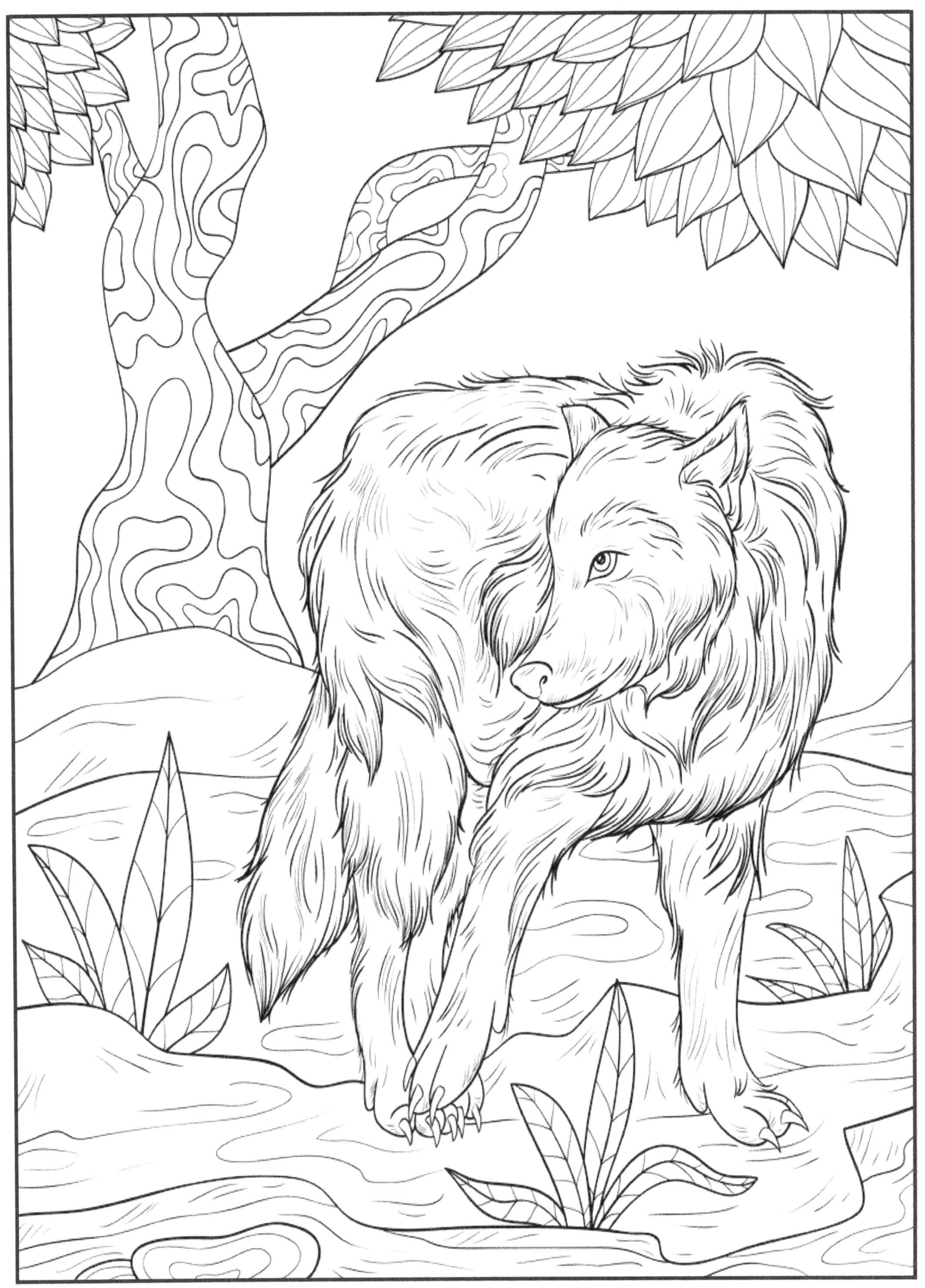

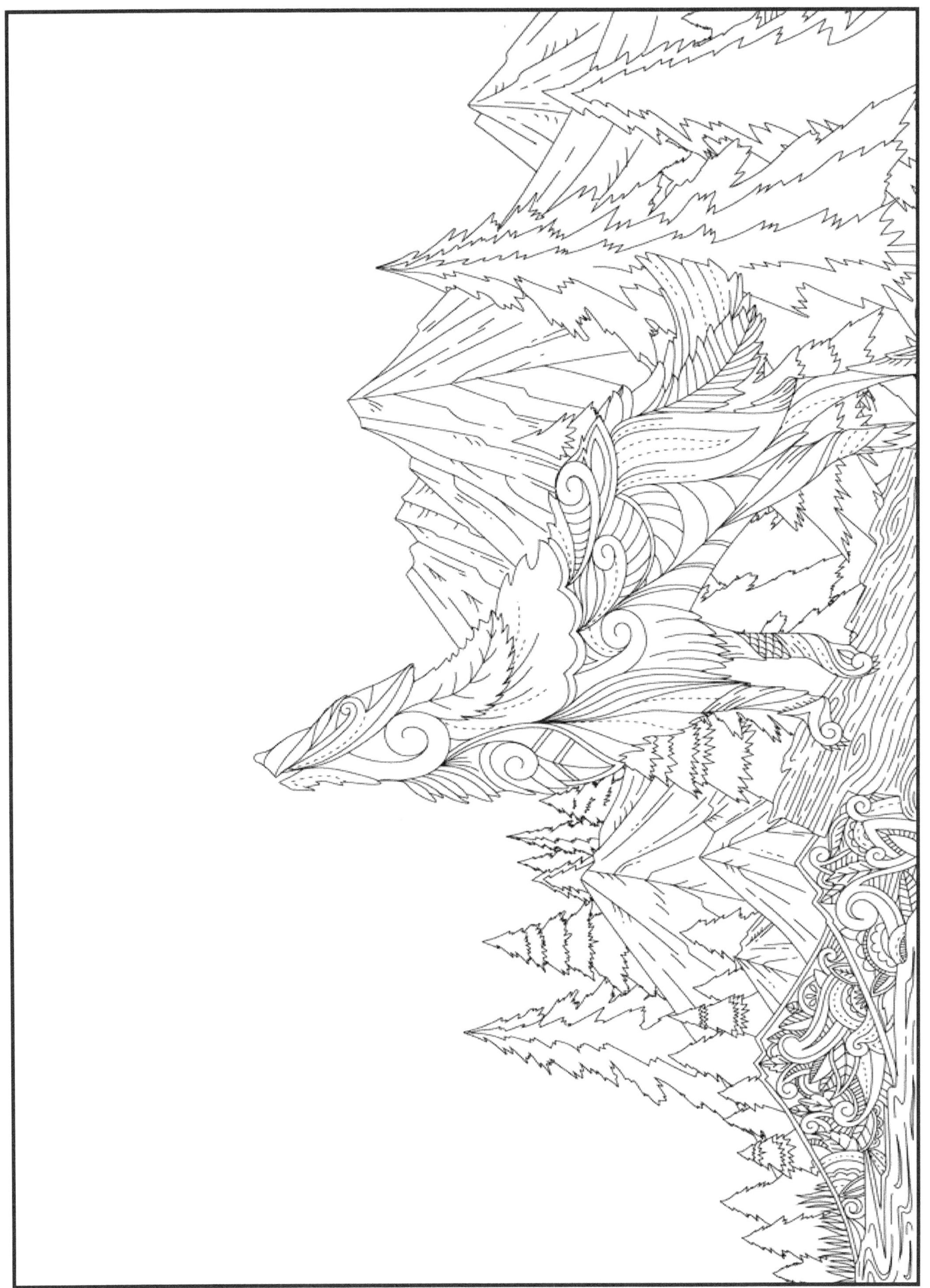

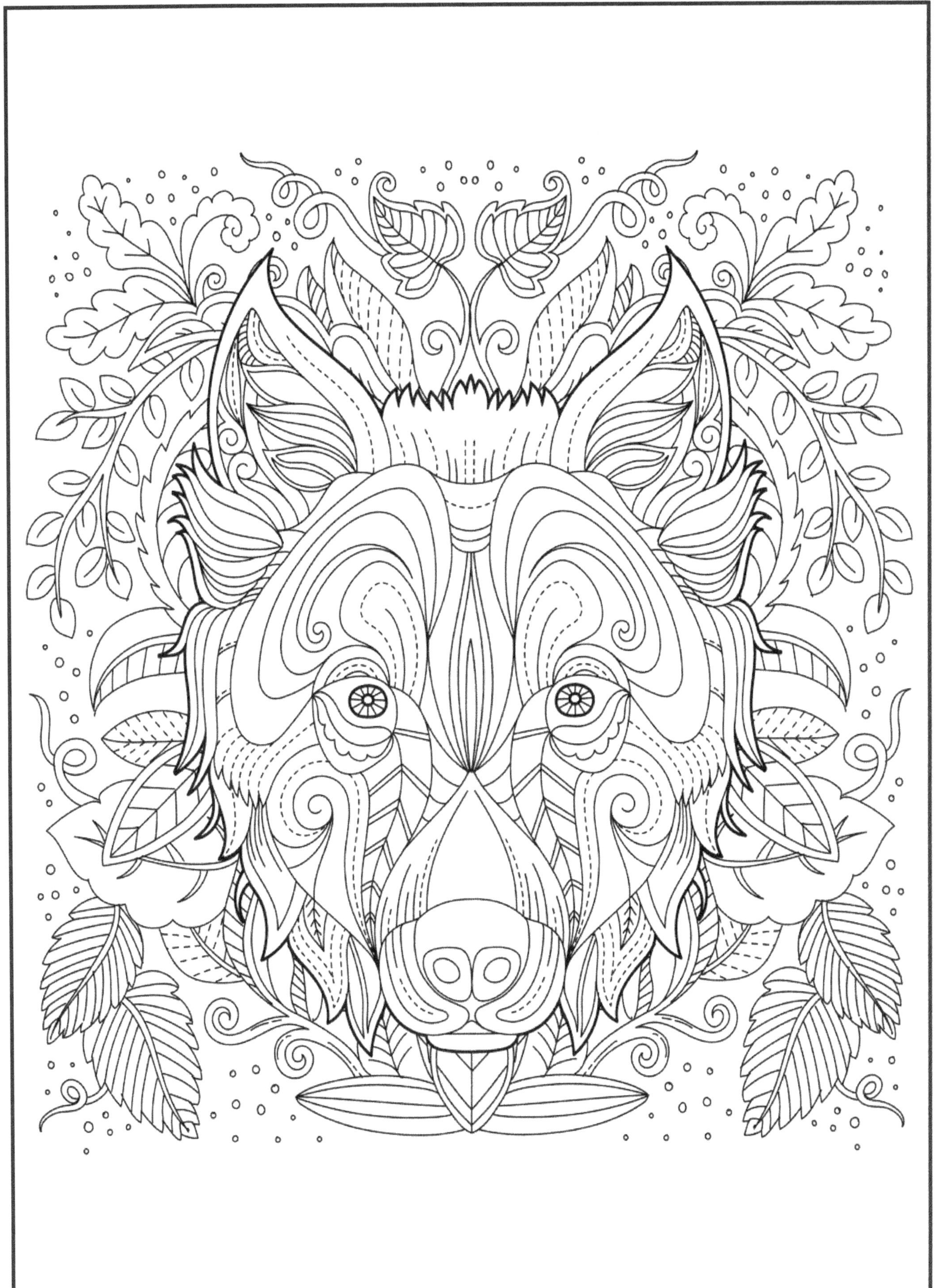

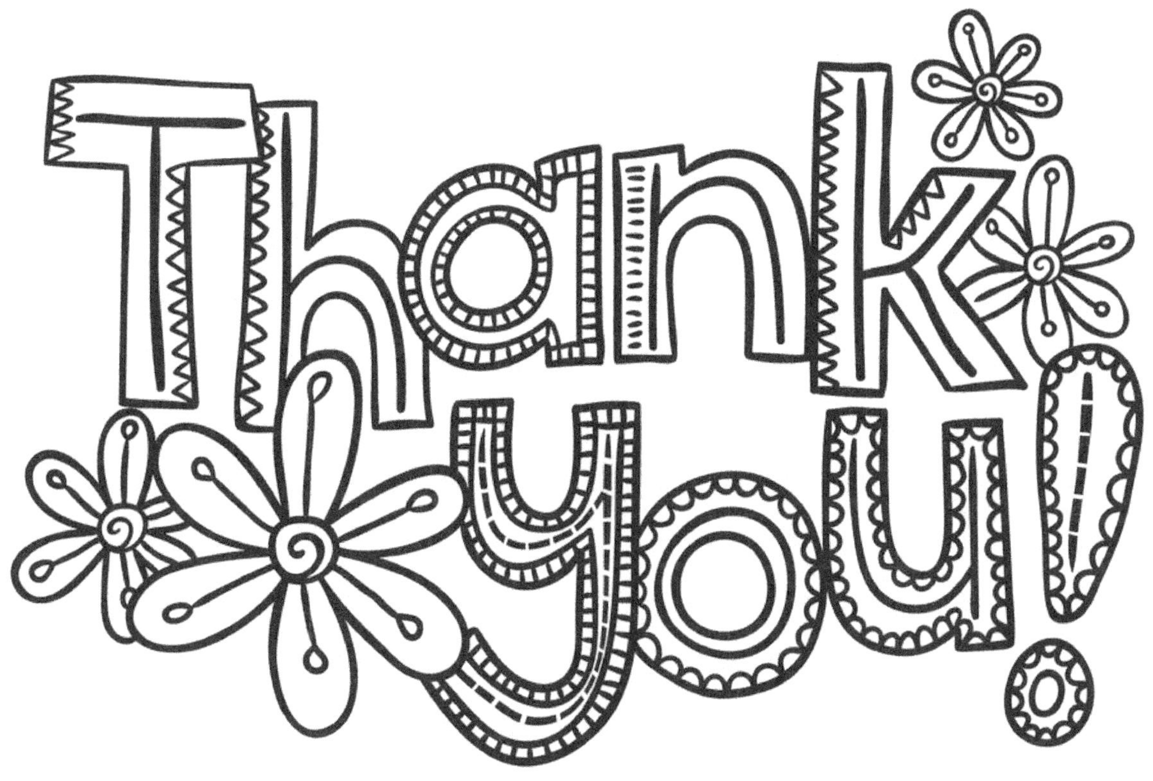

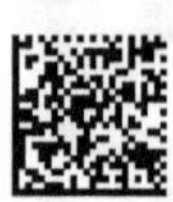